MW00883976

To Pat,
God's blessings as
you grow in His Word.
2 Peter 3:18.
Barbara Barnes

A Lady's Pocketbook Ministry

Barbara J. Barnes

WestBow Press books may be ordered through booksellers or by contacting:

WestBow Press
A Division of Thomas Nelson & Zondervan
1663 Liberty Drive
Bloomington, IN 47403
www.westbowpress.com
1 (866) 928-1240

ISBN: 978-1-4908-7482-1 (sc)
ISBN: 978-1-4908-7484-5 (hc)
ISBN: 978-1-4908-7483-8 (e)

Library of Congress Control Number: 2015904902

Print information available on the last page.

WestBow Press rev. date: 06/10/2015

Contents

Annie Strickland Lewis, my grandmother, was always willing to share God's word.

Acknowledgements

My thanks go especially to Judy Marino who has been an encouragement from the beginning, to Mike Raine who has helped with keeping scripture in context, and Janet Nusbaum for assisting with the message flow of the subject. A very special thanks to Brenda Burns for editing and teaching me computer techniques.

Dedications:

Jonathan Huggins, son, Jennifer Barrett, daughter and grandchildren Justin and Courtney Barrett.

In Memory:

Mary Frances Lewis, mother, Annie Bell Lewis, grandmother and Archie Huff, honored friend, all spiritual mentors in the practice of Christian women.

Introduction

The everyday things God has created that we can touch, see, smell, taste and hear helps us understand His inspired word and will. My inspiration for this study comes from the example Christ gave us through His life teaching about the things we see and understand with spiritual application.

In this book are many items that are found in a lady's pocketbook. Each item the lady removes from her pocketbook represents something or someone precious to her. I have taken each item to demonstrate a spiritual application such as a watch which can represent the time we spend in God's Word. We need to take advantage of every opportunity to spread the love and salvation that God has so graciously given us.

My heart's desire for this book and study of God's word is to help us see the things in our lives that will lead us in a closer walk with the Lord.

My hope and prayer is that the items displayed from this study will inspire us to think about the time we have and take advantage of every opportunity. What do we carry in our pocketbook?

Chapter 1

The first item that the lady withdrew from her pocketbook was a small, well-worn, dog- eared Bible.

Paul tells us in 2 Timothy 4:2, "Preach the word; be ready in season and out of season; reprove, rebuke, exhort, with great patience and instructions."

I almost hyperventilate every time I think someone is going to ask me something I don't think I know the answer to or where it is found in the Bible.

My first couple of years in the military, I was going to the dispensary at least two or three times a month for hyperventilation. Once it was so bad I lost the feeling in my limbs and suffered temporary loss of sight. That experience was so scary I learned quickly how to breathe into a paper bag. I carried a paper bag with me for several years to be prepared for the next time. I was amused at church one Sunday when I overheard someone mention their paper bag and thought how I had proven this over and over and happy to know that it still works. Being prepared as much as possible will help overcome whatever is troubling us in our life.

When we fail to research a physical problem and understand the reason it happens, then the problem continues and we keep having the same results. If we can't conquer our problems, we should seek medical help. This is the same with our spiritual life. We have easy access from the Bible as to how God wants us to overcome our spiritual dilemmas. We need to learn how to use the tools God has given us through His Word. It is written in Psalms 119:11, "Your word I have hidden in my heart, that I might not sin against You."

Paul writes in Ephesians 3:17 that we are to be rooted and grounded in love. Paul also tells us we are to be ready both in season and out of season. When we have God's Word hidden, grounded, and rooted in our heart with love, we will be ready. God will use us according to His purpose. Job writes these instructions in Job 22:22, "Receive, please, instruction from His mouth, and lay up His words in your heart."

Paul tells us in 2 Timothy 3:16-17, "All Scripture is inspired by God and profitable for teaching, for reproof, for correction, for training in righteousness; that the man of God may be adequate, equipped for every good work."

God has given us the answers that lead to salvation and hope of heaven. Of course, if we never research His word, we will continue to fail and those we want most to help will not be helped. We may never get but one opportunity to share the gospel and we really need to be adequately equipped when that opportunity presents itself.

We go into battle with the full amour of God as He tells us in Ephesians 6:13-17, "Therefore, take up the full armor of God, that you may be able to resist in the evil day, and having done everything to stand firm. Stand firm therefore, Having Girded Your Loins With Truth, and Having Put On The Breastplate Of Righteousness, and having Shod Your Feet With the Preparation Of The Gospel Of Peace; in addition to all, taking up the shield of faith with which you will be able to extinguish all the flaming arrows of the evil one. And take the helmet of salvation, and the sword of the Spirit, which is the word of God." **God will never leave us to fight our enemies alone.**

We read in 2 Timothy 1:7, "For God has not given us a spirit *of* timidity, but of power and love and discipline." When we know the problem and we have the solution for it, then we should be able to master it with God's help. Knowing all the right answers will not necessarily take away the fear, but it will help us to be prepared and with prayer and love we will eventually reach our goals and share the good news with those we love as well as others.

When we become children of God He expects us to multiply and share the good news everywhere we go and with everyone we meet. He gives us this commandment in Matthew 28:19-20, "Go therefore and make disciples of all the nations, baptizing them in the name of the Father and the Son and the Holy Spirit, teaching them to observe all that I commanded you; and lo I am with you always, even to the end of the age." What an awesome promise. What an awesome God, Who will deliver what He promises.

Worksheet for Chapter 1

1. Do we study daily to prepare for a Bible study?
2. Make a list of people we want to study with. Pray for the opportunity.
3. How do we achieve the goal we set to study God's Word?
4. Do we attend workshops that will help us?
5. What is your greatest fear when trying to share the gospel?
6. Do we try to take on so much that we are sure to fail?
7. Do we always ask for God's help?
8. Do we thank Him when we have completed our goal or Bible study?

We are all at different levels in our spiritual life and it may take more time for some to reach their goal than others. We should feel comfortable enough to ask others for help when we need it. Pray always and read the Bible at every opportunity. Think of times when we are waiting for something or someone and use that time to study. Do not become discouraged when we have not met our time frame, after all, it is our time frame. Just never give up and God will never give up on us.

Paul writes in Philippians 1:6, "For I am confident of this very thing, that He who began a good work in you will perfect it until the day of Christ Jesus."

Chapter 2

The second item the lady pulled from her purse was a set of keys.

Everyone has keys. We open, close, lock, and unlock something every day. We want to feel safe and secure within our homes. We want to keep our things from being stolen, thus keys become very important to us. Many times we misplace our keys and have to return to where we left them before we can continue on our journey. Having done so myself, thankfully I have family in the locksmith business as well as several family members having a duplicate. Sometimes we misplace our spiritual key and need to return to the scripture because it is the key or source that helps us back on the right track.

Peter through the Father declared to Jesus that He was the Christ, the Son of the living God. Jesus told Peter in Matthew 16:19, "And I will give you the keys of the kingdom of heaven…" After this confession, Jesus began to explain to

His disciples His mission upon earth and all the things He would suffer, even death on the cross. He taught them that He would rise on the third day and that He would return to sit at the right hand of God's throne. The disciples did not fully understand that through Christ the door of heaven would be open to all who choose to be obedient to God's Word. Jesus promised them that the believers would have a place prepared for them, in heaven with Him and the Father in John chapter 14.

So many times we turn the key to close our hearts to God's Word. Jesus spoke to the people in John 5:39-47 although they searched the scriptures thinking they had eternal life, the scripture clearly states they did not. Some people believe they understand and know what God wants without our ever studying God's Word. We are told to search the scriptures to see what is true and not trying to justify what we want it to say. In 1 John 3:17 it is written, "But whoever has this world's goods, and sees his brother in need, and shuts up *his* heart from him, how does the love of God abide in him?" Are we closed minded to our brother's need? Do we lock our love and care inside? Do we fear hurt when we open our hearts to others? Eternal life with the Father is more than worth the risk. Do others see Jesus in us when we do things for them? Maybe we should try to see through God's eyes and see what He sees in our heart.

Do we have the same love for others that God has for us? When we read of the parables of the lost sheep, lost coins, and lost son in Luke chapter 15, does our heart rejoice when all is found? God looks at the heart, so is our heart right when we give to others? Do we glorify the Father in what we do? Is our heart unlocked?

God has given us the key to enter into Christ and receive the riches of His grace and the way of salvation. Peter gives us God's way into Christ in Acts 2:38, "Then Peter said to them, Repent, and let every one of you be baptized in the name of Jesus Christ for the remission of sins, and you shall receive the gift of the Holy Spirit." The riches of God's grace are only in Christ. Baptism is the key in which we are buried to the old self and rise up out of the water a new person in Christ. God does not leave us on our own, but gives us the Holy Spirit, the comforter. His word gives us the commandments we are to live by as John writes in I John 5:3, "For this is the love of God, that we keep His commandments. And His commandments are not burdensome." Another key is found in John 14:15, "If you love Me, keep My commandments." We read in Ephesians 1:3, "Blessed be the God and Father of our Lord Jesus Christ, who has blessed us with every spiritual blessing in the heavenly places in Christ." **Our blessings are only in Christ.**

Peter writes in 2 Peter 1:5-11 how we are to grow in Christian virtue, "But also for this very reason, giving all diligence, add to your faith virtue, to virtue knowledge, to knowledge self-control, to self-control perseverance, to perseverance godliness, to godliness brotherly kindness, and to brotherly kindness love. For if these things are yours and abound, you will be neither barren nor unfruitful in the knowledge of our Lord Jesus Christ. For he who lacks these things is short-sighted, even to blindness, and has forgotten that he was cleansed from his old sins. Therefore, brethren, be even more diligent to make your call and election sure, for if you do these things you will never stumble; for so an entrance will be supplied to you abundantly into the everlasting kingdom of our Lord and Savior Jesus Christ." What a wonderful comfort to know that our God will supply all our needs, not all our wants or greed, but our daily bread.

Matthew writes in chapter 3:8, "Therefore bear fruits worthy of repentance." It is not always easy to stop doing some things that have become daily habits. Sometimes we need to examine ourselves to see if we really have repented and turned the key to lock out our old ways. We need to be around Christians that can help us with our withdrawal from our former way of life. Being in a Bible study will help us to grow in the grace and knowledge of God's word. Peter writes in 2 Peter 3:18, "But grow in the grace and knowledge of our Lord and Savior Jesus Christ. To Him be the glory both now and forever." A class for new Christians is great if your church has one. You might want to just take a correspondence course in the privacy of your home first. This will help you feel more at ease when in a classroom situation. Call and ask the minister for a Bible study or correspondence course.

Hospitality is one of the keys that opens the door to share the gospel with others. Building relationships with our friends and neighbors can help them feel secure enough to open their hearts to receive God's word. There is a saying, and I don't know from whom, 'that people don't care how much you know, until they know how much you care.' Jesus said in Matthew 25:35, "For I was hungry, and you gave Me food; I was thirsty, and you gave Me drink; I was a stranger, and you took Me in." I realize that today you cannot and should not invite just any stranger into your home, but are you inviting those you know into your homes or out for a meal? We had very little to spare in my family of eight, but my Mom opened our home to the young people for popcorn, homemade ice cream, or watermelon parties. Even though our home was small we would have thirty or more and everyone had a good time. People know when hospitality is from your heart and with love.

There is one key that we need to use every day and that is the key that locks away the wrongful use of the tongue. In James we read how destructive the tongue can be. James tells us in chapter 3:5-8, "Even so the tongue is a little member and boasts great things. See how great a forest a little fire kindles! And the tongue is a fire, a world of iniquity. The tongue is so set among our members that it defiles the whole body, and sets on fire the course of nature, and is set on fire by hell. For every kind of beasts and bird, of reptile and creature of the sea, is tamed and has been tamed by mankind. But no man can tame the tongue. It is an unruly evil, full of deadly poison." The tongue weighs less than a half pound, but destroys more lives than an atomic bomb. We need to keep our thoughts pure and then our speech will be pure. Our heart should be filled with the Word of God so we must study and be ready to say and do the right thing. This will help us avoid the evil that takes away our joy in Christ. We read in Proverbs 23:7, "For as he thinks in his heart, so is he..." We read in Proverbs 18:21, "Death and life are in the power of the tongue..."

I know we have all heard the saying that sticks and stones may break my bones, but words can never hurt me. This is not a true saying. As it is written, words can have the power of life or death over us. Words are made into law that can take away some of our freedoms, even trying to tell us how we can worship God and how we can no longer use some of God's Word.

Just as we should never leave home without our key, we should never leave without God's key that opens our heart and shares the Good News with others. Start each day in prayer for an opportunity to be opened for you. Remember in Proverbs 25:11, "A word fitly spoken is like apples of gold in settings of silver." God be with you as you share His message with others.

Worksheet for Chapter 2

1. How can we open our door so others can come in?
2. Why do we pray before we read the scriptures?
3. Do we open our mind when we read the scriptures?
4. What value do we place on Christ and His promises?
5. Do we still have things in our life that need repentance?
6. Are we adding the virtues needed to become a fruit bearing Christian?
7. Give two scriptures why we trust God to supply all our needs.
8. How does God use us with the sharing of His word with others?

Remember that "no one cares how much you know until they know how much you care." Many times we are told to use key words or thoughts to remember names or information. Getting in the habit of thinking how we are to respond to someone when we have the opportunity is well worth the effort. The joy it brings to others will give us the inspiration to continue passing on the Good News to all we meet. **God is always there for you**.

"I can do all things through Christ who strengthens me." Philippians 4:13

Chapter 3

The third item the lady removed from her pocketbook was a small photo album. The first photos were of her family.

There is no greater gift than the gift of God's Son. The value of the gift one gives is not only in the gift, but the value is also in the heart of the giver. God's gift to us, His only begotten Son was Love from the heart of God to us His creation. Do we give to others out of obligation or out of love? We read of God's love in John 13:34-35,"A new commandment I give to you, that you Love one another; as I have loved you, that you also love one another. By this all will know that you are My disciples, if you have love for one another."

Most everyone keeps their family photos within close reach. It helps to bring the memories of those we love or have loved close in our heart. The photos remind us of how much we love and how much we are loved. John writes in 1 John 4:11, "Beloved, if God so loved us, we also ought to love one another." We love our family with an earthly love and this love helps us relate to the love that the Father has for us. "We love Him because He first loved us." 1 John 4:19. Paul instructs us in Ephesians 5:1-2, "Therefore, be imitators of God, as dear children; and walk in love, as Christ also has loved us and given Himself for us, an offering and a sacrifice to God for a sweet-smelling aroma." Do we have the love that offers a sweet aroma to God? Paul writes in 1 Corinthians 13:13, "And now abide faith, hope, love, these three, but the greatest of these is love." Also, Paul writes in 1 Corinthians 13:1, "Though I speak with the tongues of men and of angels, but have not love, I have become sounding brass or a clanging cymbal." There is no doubt about it; we must have love in our heart to be pleasing to God. Hopefully we learn about love from our family.

First we must love God above all others. We read in 1 John 4:16, "And we have known and believed the love that God has for us. God is love, and he who abides in love abides in God and God in him." We are to put God first in our lives as He tells us in Mark 12:30, "And you shall love the Lord your God with all your heart, with all your soul, with all your mind, and with all your strength." Why are we to always put God first in our life? This is found in John 3:16, "For God so loved the world that He gave His only begotten Son, that whoever believes in Him should not perish, but have everlasting life." God loved us so much He has given us the sacrifice of His Son through His blood we can receive a crown of life and eternity in heaven. We want our children to love us and as His children, He wants us to love Him.

Then, there is another special love in our life. The love we receive as children from our parents is with us throughout our lives, even after they are gone. My mother died a few years ago and I thank God every day for the influence of her love. The love she showed my brothers and me was not just earthly love, but the love she had for God.

She made sure we knew the love of the Father. All six of her children were baptized into Christ; at this time I am the only one that remains faithful. Love needs to grow and increase if we are to stay faithful. God gives a promise to children that are obedient to their parents in Ephesians 6:1-2, "Children, obey your parents in the Lord, for this is right. Honor your Father and Mother which is the first commandment with a promise; that it may be well with you, and that you may live long on the earth."

Loving my mother was not difficult because she returned my love, but it was different with my dad. My dad drank a lot and never returned love openly; however, at the end of his life when he had stopped drinking, he told me that he loved me. We prayed together and I forgave him for not being able to show love earlier in my life. When God can forgive, then how can we keep our forgiveness from others? We desperately want that love and we need it. Knowing the love of our heavenly Father can help us in our love one for another. **God knows when it is from our heart.** We read in Romans 12:9, "Let love be without hypocrisy. Abhor what is evil. Cling to what is good." Sometimes we really have to pray and allow God to help us in loving some people. We must remember that we are not always lovable ourselves. "If it is possible, as much as depends on you, live peaceably with all men." Romans 12:18

There is also a love that comes when we are adults; it is the love of husband and wife. God says in Matthew 19:5, "…, For this reason a man shall leave his father and mother and be joined to his wife, and the two shall become one flesh." God instructs the wife and the husband on how to love one another in Ephesians 5:22-25, "Wives, submit to your own husbands, as to the Lord. For the husband is the head of the wife, as also Christ is the head of the church; and He is the Savior of the body. Therefore, just as the church is subject to Christ, so let the wives be to their own husbands in everything. Husbands, love your wives, just as Christ also loved the church and gave Himself for her."

We are to love each other as if it is unto the Lord. The love of husband and wife is a very special love that should endure until death. We must pray to choose the right person to marry and spend our life with him/her. Being unequally yoked can cause much heartache and hardship. I write from experience in my own marriage. Never marry someone that you plan to change. Change is up to the individual. Sometimes your life will be an influence for your mate to accept Christ and this will be worth every sacrifice you make to bring this about. Peter writes in 1 Peter 3:1, "Wives, likewise, be submissive to your own husbands, that even if some do not obey the word, they, without a word, may be won by the conduct of their wives." There is no greater earthly love than that of a loving husband and wife. Keeping God first in your marriage will help keep you together for a life time. How wonderful to grow together in God's grace. A good marriage does not just happen. There is much give and take from both sides, but with love you will make it. Just remember to practice the principles of Godly living and never comprise that. A good passage to remember is found in 1 Corinthians 13:4-7, "Love suffers long and is kind; love does not envy; love does not parade itself, it is not puffed up; does not behave rudely, does not seek its own, is not provoked, thinks no evil; does not rejoice in iniquity, but rejoices in the truth; bears all things, believes all things, hopes all things, endures all things." Practicing this formula will keep your love forever burning brightly throughout your marriage. 50% will give only half of something. **Each one needs to give 100% to each other**.

Another love is the love we have for our children when we become parents. It is a special love and we want to help our children have the best of life. We want them to be strong and faithful in the Lord. Solomon wrote in Proverbs 22:6, "Train up a child in the way he should go, And when he is old he will not depart from it." Paul writes this to the fathers in Ephesians 6:4, "And you, fathers, do not provoke your children to wrath, but bring them up in the training and admonition of the Lord." In the Old Testament the Jews were to teach their children in this way in Deuteronomy 6:6-7, "And these words which I command you today shall be on your heart. You shall teach them diligently to your children, and shall talk to them when you sit in your house, and when you walk by the way, and when you lie down, and when you rise up." We are to teach and be an example for our children in every way as God has commanded. What a blessing God has challenged us with through His word as we grow and mature in our faith. We will fail from time to time, but helping our children to have the trust and love for God in their lives will keep us diligent in our efforts to bring this about. **The greatest gift a parent can give their child is to be a loving and faithful example in their walk of faith in Christ.** Older women are to teach the younger women to love their children in Titus 2:4.

There are times when we need to observe our children closely and learn from them. God said to His disciples in Matthew 18:1-5, "At that time the disciples came to Jesus, saying," 'Who then is greatest in the kingdom of heaven?" Then Jesus called a little child to Him, set him in the midst of them, and said, "Assuredly, I say to you, unless you are converted and become as little children, you will by no means enter the kingdom of heaven. "Therefore whoever humbles himself as this little child is the greatest in the kingdom of heaven. "Whoever receives one little child like this in My name receives Me." Children depend and trust us to do the very best for them, most of the time without question. We must humble ourselves and have that dependence and trust in God without question or doubt.

Worksheet for Chapter 3

1. Make a list of ways to share God's love.
2. Write ways God can help us be more loving.
3. What are some things that will help keep God first in our lives?
4. Discuss opportunities where we can be of help to others.
5. List some of your husband's good qualities.
6. List some of the good qualities of your children.
7. What are some good qualities of our parents that have influenced us?
8. What are some ways we can help each other teach?

We love the Lord and we cherish our family.
"Thanks be to God for His indescribable gift." 2 Corinthians 9:15

Chapter 4

The lady continued to look at her photo album of her friends she loved that had touched her life.

We find in Proverbs 17:17a, "A friend loves at all times..." This is so true when your friend is truly a close friend. I always think of Archie Huff when I think of a friend that loves at all times. She was my spiritual mentor during a time in my life when I really needed a friend in Christ. God has blessed my life with many dear and wonderful friends. Friends see the potential in us, not our problems. "As iron sharpens iron, so a man sharpens the countenance of his friend." Proverbs 27:17

Friends that are members of the body of Christ are the most cherished friends. Abraham was called a friend of God. What a blessing. God says we can be a friend also in John 15:14, "You are My friends, if you do whatever I command you." He tells us the love of a friend in John 15:13, "Greater love has no one than this, than to lay down one's life for his friends." I am reminded of our soldiers that lay down their lives for ours daily. It brings tears to my eyes and a thankful heart for their willingness to do this so we can continue to enjoy our freedom. Having had a grand-niece in Iraq kept me in prayer for her as well as others for a safe return. A truly close friend is one you can always depend on no matter what, just like Jesus does in the song we sing "What a Friend we have in Jesus." We share our secrets with a friend who will keep them, just like God when he hears our prayers. A friend prays for you and with you. I recall a verse that to have a good friend, you need to be one. "A man who has friends must himself be friendly, but there is a friend who sticks closer than a brother." Proverbs 18:24

Our first commandment is to Love God with all our heart, soul, mind and strength. Then we are commanded to love our neighbors as ourselves in Mark 12:31, "And the second, like it, is this, 'You shall love your neighbor as yourself.' There is no other commandment greater than these." First we are to love God and then to love our neighbor. Is our neighbor just the people who live the closest to us? Many passages give us insight as to who our neighbors are. One passage is found in Galatians 6:10, "Therefore, as we have opportunity, let us do good to all, especially to those who are of the household of faith." This lets us know that we are to put the body of Christ first, also, we are to do good for any who are in need. Jesus tells a parable that demonstrates who our neighbor is in Luke 10:29-37, the good Samaritan. Are we the one who stops to help another or are we the one that passes by and leaves it to someone else? Paul writes in 1 Corinthians 10:24 "Let no one seek his own, but each one the other's wellbeing." I remember one time when my mother told me about a family in the community who had lost their home in a fire. My mother believed she should help anyone in time of need and she did regardless of any help from others. My mother was a great example of giving to others at every opportunity as written in Galatians 6:10. Everything we have is from God and is to be used according to His purpose using sound judgment. When we give it is no longer up to us, it is in God's hand.

It is not ours to judge when God has placed someone in our path in need of things we can supply. **When we give we should do it because of who we are and not for whom they are.** We should be grateful enough because we are God's children and He supplies our needs when we ask. As His children, He expects no less from us. We should always thank God for loving us enough to put others in our life to help and share our blessings. God is the one who rewards us. Sometimes we reason that since the church 'collectively' should do it or has done it, we are relieved of our individual responsibility. This never relieves one from individual obligations. We are to do all we can, and then some.

The second part of that verse tells us we are to love ourselves. It would be hard to have love for others when we have little to offer. We must feel good about ourselves and have the confidence that we can love others. Our value and worth as individuals is seen in how much God paid through the shedding of Christ's blood. God values us enough that he gave His loving precious Son so that we could have the hope of heaven. Love is active and needs to be shared. I remember a song we use to sing at the Christian school my children attended. A few of the words went like this, "love is like a lucky penny, hold on tight and you won't have any, give it away and you will end up having more." We are not to have a selfish love or false pride, but genuine love. We are to be cheerful in our giving to God and others. There is a saying I have heard that goes like this, "God doesn't make junk." We are God's creation and He loves us. God gave His Son for us even while we were sinners. That makes us very valuable to Him. Do we feel valued? What we feel in our hearts and the happiness that we have is not dependent upon someone else; it is within each of us. I have a little picture and saying on my refrigerator that Abraham Lincoln wrote, "Most folks are about as happy as they make up their minds to be." We read in Proverbs 23:7a, "For as he thinks in his heart, so is he..."

Paul writes in Philippians 4:8, "Finally, brethren, whatever things are true, whatever things are noble, whatever things are just, whatever things are pure, whatever things are lovely, whatever things are of good report, if there is any virtue and if there is anything praise-worthy- meditate on these things." **We must get our thinking and heart right with God.** Think about some things you can change in your life that will help you love yourself more.

Our next form of love that God asks us to have in our life is rather hard at times and we really need to concentrate and pray about it. Jesus tells His disciples in Luke 6:27-32, "But I say to you who hear: Love your enemies, do good to those who hate you, bless those who curse you, and pray for those who spitefully use you. To him who strikes you on the one cheek, offer the other also. And from him, who takes away your cloak, do not withhold your tunic either. Give to everyone who asks of you. And from him who takes away your goods do not ask them back. And just as you want men to do to you, you also do to them likewise. But if you love those who love you, what credit is that to you? For even the sinners love those who love them." Loving our enemies has far more to do with who we are rather than who they are.

Jesus went to the cross for the sins of everyone. We are so grateful for the grace of God and the blood of Christ that washes our sins away that we want everyone to have that opportunity, even our enemies. Jesus tells us in Matthew 5:11-12, "Blessed are you when they revile and persecute you, and say all kinds of evil against you falsely for My sake. Rejoice and be exceedingly glad, for great is your reward in heaven, for so they persecuted the prophets who were before you."

There are many who are still persecuted for teaching the gospel in several countries, even to the point of death. I know of some who have been subjected to these hardships, but not in this country. It seems at times that our brethren can cause some of our biggest hardships. Our enemies are those who want to separate us from our love for God. Jesus says that anyone who is not for Me is against Me in Matthew 12:30. We must ask God to help us do as He tells us in Luke 6:27-28, "But I say to you who hear: Love your enemies, do good to those who hate you, bless those who curse you, and pray for those who spitefully use you." Hate will eat our heart, soul, and take away our joy. It is self-defeating and profits nothing. When someone has done you wrong, praying for them is not usually your first response. Jesus prayed for those who crucified Him in Luke 23:34, "Then Jesus said, "Father, forgive them, for they do not know what they do." And they divided His garments and cast lots." This is so true of those who do not know the love of God. When we are wronged and we respond back in the wrong way, how can we ever hope to bring that person to Christ? We may not be able to share the gospel with them, but we can certainly pray for their salvation. Their sins can be forgiven by God just as ours have been. Paul writes in Ephesians 2:8-9, "For by grace you have been saved through faith, and that not of yourselves, it is the gift of God; not of works, lest anyone should boast."

God wants our love for Him to be so great that we see and understand the need for Christ in everyone's life. We may be the planters of the seed and never see the acceptance of Christ in those we teach. Just remember, unless the seed is planted God's word will not be heard, so rejoice in your heart when you have sown the seed. **It is God's word that convicts the heart.** We are only the vessel that delivers the message. There is nothing in this world that can compare to being a Christian and to know that you are never alone. Jesus spoke these words in Luke 19:10, "But the Son of Man has come to seek and to save that which was lost." **Our mission is to seek the lost, God will do the saving.**

Worksheet for chapter 4

1. What makes our best friend our friend?
2. Who are some of our closest friends?
3. List qualities that make a friend, a friend.
4. What helps us love ourselves more?
5. Discuss ways we can reach out to our friends and neighbors.
6. What are ways we can help others to know the love of God?
7. What should our attitude be toward our enemies?

"Let all that you do be done in love." 1 Corinthians 16:14

Chapter 5

Next the little lady removed a small pendant watch wrapped in a smooth velvet cloth. This was a prized possession given to her by her children.

Time and time again we try to stretch a day into more than twenty-four hours. We try to cram every second into two more seconds, as if we really could. I believe God made us to fit into a twenty-four hour day and not the other way around. It is up to each of us as to how we are to exchange our time and make the most of it. You have heard and it is so true that time does not wait for anyone. I am so guilty of letting time pass by and thinking I will get around to it eventually. It is gone, never to be recovered. Pray each morning that you will spend the day praising God and using every minute with planned purpose.

God has set a time for us to worship Him in Spirit and Truth. Paul writes in Acts 20:7a; "Now on the first day of the week, when the disciples came together to break bread…"

We should never have to think about where we will be on Sunday morning, unless we have to work a morning shift or we have an emergency. Not only do we need to attend worship service, but we need to be on time. We never want God to be late with the things we ask of Him. God comes first and if we don't put Him first, then we are going to lose out on that time called eternity in Heaven. God makes it very clear in Mark 12:30, "And you shall love the Lord your God with all your heart, with all your soul, with all your mind, and with all your strength. This is the first commandment." God should be number one in our life. Matthew writes in Matthew 6:33; "But seek first the kingdom of God and His righteousness, and all these things shall be added to you." Many excuses for not attending have been made, but very few are really valid or justified according to scripture. God knows the reason when we miss. We should be concerned about our self because we are the one who will stand before God in the Day of Judgment. Paul writes in 2 Corinthians 5:10; "For we must all appear before the judgment seat of Christ, that each one may receive the things done in the body, according to what he has done whether good or bad." God's word is our spiritual food and my personal opinion is some of us are starving and don't know it. Our time may not only benefit us in worship service, but we may be helping a weaker brother/sister be stronger. God is counting on our love because He has blessed us and given us hope through Christ, His beloved Son.

The time we spend with our loved ones is measured by the influence we leave when we are gone. John writes in Revelation 14:13; "Then I heard a voice from heaven saying to me, "Write: 'Blessed are the dead who die in the Lord from now on." "Yes," says the Spirit, "that they may rest from their labors and their works follow them." We can always change while we are alive, but when we die only our influence will remain to guide those we love good or bad. Time is the same for every one of us and it is up to us to use it in the way that God has planned.

Jesus told his disciples that His time was fleeing in John 9:4, "I must work the works of Him who sent Me while it is day, the night is coming when no one can work." Jesus was given a time to fulfill the promise God had made from the beginning of time, to bring about the redemption of mankind. Whatever time we are given, we are to work with all our might as unto the Lord. God gives us a time for sowing His word and if we don't use that time, then the reaping will not be fruitful and we will be accountable like the one talent man we read about in Matthew 25:26-28.

Solomon gives us wisdom on time as he writes in Ecclesiastes 3:1-8, "In everything there is a season, a time for every purpose under heaven; a time to be born, and a time to die; a time to plant, and a time to pluck what is planted; a time to kill, and a time to heal; a time to break down, and a time to build up; a time to weep, and a time to laugh; a time to mourn, and a time to dance; a time to cast away stones, and a time to gather stones; a time to embrace, and a time to refrain from embracing; a time to gain, and a time to lose; a time to keep, and a time to throw away; a time to tear, and a time to sew; a time to keep silence, and a time to speak; a time to love, and a time to hate; a time of war, and a time of peace."

Many who know the truth are like Felix after Paul had preached to him about Christ. We think there will always be time as did Felix when he said to Paul in Acts 24:25, "Now as he reasoned about righteousness, self-control, and the judgment to come, Felix was afraid and answered "Go away for now; when I have a convenient time I will call for you" Our salvation does not depend on our convenience. Paul writes to the Corinthians and tells them in 2 Corinthians 6:2b, "…Behold, now is the accepted time, behold, now is the day of salvation." Tomorrow may be too late!

There is a popular song that says time is on our side. This is not true concerning our spiritual life. We read of the foolish rich man that thought he had all the time to revel in his selfishness, but it did not happen. As we read in Luke 12:19:20, "And I will say to my soul, "Soul, you have many goods laid up for many years; take your ease, eat, drink, and be merry', but God said to him, 'Fool! This night your soul will be required of you; then whose will those things be which you have provided?' There is no time off or retirement in God's kingdom. How we spend our time is important not only for our self but for others. If we miss an opportunity to help someone who is seeking Christ we may never get another chance and they may never be at that place again. **We have a mission and we need to be ready.**

What do we give in exchange for our time? Could the lack of time management cost us our soul? Jesus said in Matthew 16:26, "For what profit is it to a man if he gains the whole world, and loses his own soul? Or what will a man give in exchange for his soul?" Take time for God not only in prayer, but in scripture.

Next you need to take time for your family. I remember when my daughter was two or three and she would try to get her dad's attention while he was reading the morning paper. He would brush her off and say 'later'. One day I stood in front of my daughter and said to my husband that later his daughter may not want her dad's attention. The paper was cancelled the next day. Our children want our approval and our attention. When we neglect to do so, then they are likely to look in places and to people that will take them away from us. Paul writes in Ephesians 6:4, "And you fathers, do not provoke your children to wrath, but bring them up in the training and admonition of the Lord." You may think you have time, but believe me, children grow up fast and then we have lost that precious time with them. Teach them in a way that will secure them in their faith and not yours. If it is your faith living in them, then when they are away from you it will be hard for them to remain faithful. Many times I wish I could have a do over with my children and prepare them better in God's Word. Too many times we take time away from our family and spend it with others. When my grandchildren want to read or tell me something, I stop and take the time to listen. I learned that lesson from not taking enough time with my children.

In today's world both parents usually are working outside of the home. Unfortunately most young couples today are trying to keep their heads above water with their finances. The important thing to remember is that working for what you need is the right thing to do. Paul writes in 2 Thessalonians 3:10, "For even when we were with you, we commanded you this: If anyone will not work, neither shall he eat." However when you work more hours than required so you can give your family more things, you usually lose more than you gain. Things are of no value if we lose those closest to us and we can never make up lost time. I must confess that I have been guilty of that myself. Place this scripture somewhere you can see it and say it often. "But seek first the kingdom of God and His righteousness, and all these things shall be added to you. Therefore do not worry about tomorrow, for tomorrow will worry about its own things. Sufficient for the day is its own trouble." Matthew 6:33-34. **Things can be replaced with time, but time cannot be replaced.** Always tell those you love that you love them. Don't let time pass and you never get the chance. Take the time to correct any wrongs you have done to your family, friends or anyone no matter who was at fault. Make peace while you still have the time to do so. Acknowledge your wrong, apologize for the wrong, and if possible make it right. How we can make it right is a lesson we can all learn and practice.

Spending time with friends is great and we need to spend time with them. However, if we neglect our families to do so, then we need to re-think the situation. We should be able to make plans with our families and our friends that does not infringe upon each other. Our families are a blessing here on earth and we want them to be in heaven with us. They are the ones we will most influence and they are the ones we want most to be children of God.

My life has been blessed by so many dear and close friends. Friendship needs time also to grow and mature. Of course, if you are married, your spouse should be your best friend. Women more so than men seek to have close friends that they can spend time with for encouragement, support, a listening ear, and shopping. I always think of David and Jonathan when I think of friendship. My son's name is Jonathan for that reason. God has given us many passages about friends and friendship. We find in Proverbs 17:17, "A friend loves at all times, and a brother is born for adversity." Proverbs 18:24. "A man who has friends must himself be friendly, but there is a friend who sticks closer than a brother." Jesus tells how we are His friends in John 15:14, "You are My friends if you do whatever I command you."

It takes time to develop a true, long-lasting friendship. It takes time to know God. We need to take the time to learn the scriptures so we can have the right relationship with our Father. **How awesome to be a friend of God**. James writes in James 2:23; "And the scripture was fulfilled which says, "Abraham believed God, and it was accounted to him for righteousness." And he was called the friend of God." I have lost some of my dearest friends and I think of so many things I wish I had thought to say and do with them. One of my best friends, my mother, is at the top of my list. Telling my children how much I love and appreciate them comes from my not telling my mother more often my love for her. Jesus tells us in John 14:15; "If you love Me, keep My commandments." No matter how much I wish I had been a better mother for my children when they were young that time is gone. Now all I can do is be thankful for the time left to influence my children for God.

When we think of all the things we need to do and the people we need to help, it does not seem to be enough time in the twenty-four hours given us each day. That is why we need to plan our time. Most of us are list makers and this helps to keep track of our time each day. Planning our time for different projects and goals will keep us from losing track of time that can bring about frustration at the end of the day. Always take time to pray for your day. Allow some time to take a breath as you plunge into your daily activities.

We need to remember to take some time for our self. We are so busy with others that we sometimes neglect ourselves. Try to start each day with some quiet time and prayer, even if it means you need to wake up earlier. Once your day starts it's like a ball going downhill and it is hard to stop and smell the flowers as the saying goes. God wants us to have a happy life being His children. How we view our self affects all the areas of our life. Paul writes in Philippians 4:4, "Rejoice in the Lord always. Again I will say, rejoice!" God tells us to love our neighbors as we love ourselves.

Taking time and being happy about ourselves will help us accomplish more and benefit our health. We read in Matthew chapter 5, happiness is a by-product of Holiness with which God blesses us.. There are things and people who take your time and drag you down. Don't allow the negative things to overcome your optimistic attitude. Sometimes we have to make new friends that will help lift us up and let others go. I always think of what John wrote in 1 John 4:4, "You are of God, little children, and have overcome them, because He who is in you is greater than he who is in the world." Time is not on our side, but God is.

Worksheet for Chapter 5

1. Why is it important to attend worship service?
2. How often are we spending time with God?
3. What are some of the reasons why we need to attend Bible Class?
4. Do we spend enough time in prayer?
5. What are the benefits of studying the Bible?
6. How should we spend time with our family?
7. Do we take time for our self?
8. When you ask for God's help, are you giving Him time to answer?

Remember that God's time is not our time and He is always available.

"Therefore humble yourselves under the mighty hand of God, that He may exalt you in due time."1 Peter 5:6

Chapter 6

The little lady reached into her pocketbook and drew out her eye glasses. "My, my I should have had these on all the time; I can see things much clearer now.

We know that we cannot see God even with the strongest of glasses. It is not with our eyes that we see God. How can we see God? Jesus said in Matthew 5:8, "Blessed are the pure in heart, for they shall see God." This is not with the optic eye but when we are pure in heart, in attitude, and with faith, we can see and know who our God is. The disciples of Jesus ask Him this very question in John 14:7-11, "If you had known Me, you would have known My Father also; and from now on you know Him and have seen Him." Philip said to Him, "Lord, show us the Father, and it is sufficient for us." Jesus said to him, "Have I been with you so long, and yet you have not known Me, Philip? He who has seen Me has seen the Father; so how can you say, 'Show us the Father'? Do you not believe that I am in the Father, and the Father in Me? The words that I speak to you I do not speak on My own authority; but the Father who dwells in Me does the works. Believe Me that I am in the Father and the Father in Me, or else believe Me for the sake of the works themselves." Jesus lets us know that He has the authority and power of God. God warned many times that to see Him would surely bring death. God sending Jesus was the perfect way for Him to converse with man on man's level and for man to see the power and love of God.

Would we have been any more aware of whom Jesus was than the disciples who were with Him during His life on earth? Maybe we would be more like Thomas when Jesus appeared to the disciples after He had risen from the grave. We find this account in John 20:27-29, "Then He said to Thomas, 'Reach your finger here and look at My hands; and reach your hand here, and put it into My side. Do not be unbelieving, but believing' And Thomas answered and said to Him, 'My Lord and my God!' Jesus said to him, "Thomas, because you have seen Me, you have believed. Blessed are those who have not seen and yet have believed." What a wonderful assurance for us who believe and have not seen with our eyes, but with our hearts.

God has given us a commandment that John writes in I John 4:20-21, "If someone says, 'I love God,' and hates his brother, he is a liar; for he who does not love his brother whom he has seen, how can he love God whom he has not seen?' And this commandment we have from Him; that he who loves God must love his brother also." The world continues to try and disprove our faith by proving there is no God. We read in Psalms 53:1a, "The fool has said in his heart, there is no God…" The world does not want God because then they would become accountable for their actions. If there is no God then there is no punishment and you would not have to do right by others. God is love, so if there is no God, then where would love be?

A Christian does not need the world to prove anything because our faith is based on God's Word and the love we see in each other. The evidence of God is everywhere. We have to have faith as it is written in Hebrews 11:6, "But without faith it is impossible to please Him, for he who comes to God must believe that He is, and that He is a rewarder of those who diligently seek Him." We read in Hebrews 11:1, "Now faith is the substance of things hoped for, the evidence of things not seen."

We remember previously what Jesus told Thomas in John 20:29, that we are blessed because of our faith in the fact that we have not physically seen Jesus. Sight takes away the hope, faith, and love for something we wanted when we receive it. Take away any one of these three and you can destroy a person. Without love shown to infants they can die. Paul writes in I Corinthians 13 that without love we are nothing. Remove the faith you have in someone you love and you withdraw and become despondent. Take away hope and you can create a prevailing mood for suicide. We can see clearly that these three are very significant for our salvation. **It is the grace of God that saves us.** We read in Ephesians 2:8, "For by grace you have been saved through faith, and that not of yourselves; it is the gift of God."

Our relationship with God should be evident to everyone who knows us. God tells us through the writings of Paul in 2 Corinthians 2:15, "For we are to God the fragrance of Christ among those who are being saved and among those who are perishing." He also tells us in 2 Corinthians 3:2, "You are our epistle written in our hearts, known and read by all men." **Our faith in God is our life, not a part of it.** God sees everything we do, everything done to us, hears everything we say, and everything we hear. When we are in darkness, it is because we have removed ourselves from His light and we are no longer abiding in Him. We need to do as David did in Psalm 119:105, "Your word is a lamp to my feet, and a light to my path." We need to pray and return to the light of God's Word. God is always watching for our return, just like the father of the prodigal son in Luke 15. It should be a comfort and an assurance to know God watches over us.

God does not see our sin once He has forgiven us. We find in 1 John 1:9, "If we confess our sins, He is faithful and just to forgive us our sins and to cleanse us from all unrighteousness." Isaiah writes in Isaiah 1:18, "Come now, and let us reason together, says the Lord, though your sins are like scarlet, they shall be as white as snow; though they are red like crimson, they shall be as wool." Do we still see our sin? We must forgive ourselves or God will not be able to use us in His plan. We must also forgive those who sin against us. Just stop forgiving people when you want God to stop forgiving you. The unforgiving heart is a heart that does not forgive and is in danger. Jesus tells us in Matthew 23:27, "Woe to you, scribes and Pharisees, hypocrites! For you are like whitewashed tombs which indeed appear beautiful outwardly, but inside they are full of dead men's bones and all uncleanness."

After Jesus told the disciples how to pray to God, He also told them to forgive others in Matthew 6:14-15, "For if you forgive men their trespasses, your heavenly Father will also forgive you. But if you do not forgive men their trespasses, neither will your Father forgive your trespasses." Do others see a forgiving heart in us? Can we see a change in ourselves? Ephesians 4:32, "And be kind to one another, tender-hearted, forgiving one another, even as God in Christ also forgave you." We do not have the option to pick and choose those we forgive and God has not set a limit on how many times we are to forgive others. God does tell us we are to forgive seventy times seven. **Our lives should always reflect a forgiving spirit.**

We have heard many times to not judge a book by its cover. We had a beautiful oak tree by the side of our patio. One day when looking outside the tree started falling toward the house. Later we learned that the beautiful oak was rotten on the inside. It stood tall for many years, but once the inside became infected and was not treated, it died from the inside out. Man sees the outside but God sees the inside. Those who are around us will soon see if we are sincere of heart. It seems that almost anything can bring a song to mind and this lesson causes me to think of the song, 'Let the Beauty of Jesus be seen in me'. God tells us how we are to be seen in Matthew 5:14-16, "You are the light of the world. A city that is set on a hill cannot be hidden. Nor do they light a lamp and put it under a basket, but on a lampstand, and it gives light to all who are in the house. Let your light so shine before men, that they may see your good works and glorify your Father in heaven." We are to let others see Christ living in our lives and bring glory to God.

Many of the early Christians were giving preference to members by elevating people of greater means to higher status than others in the assembly. The ones giving the preference were not doing this out of the kindness of their heart. You didn't need eyeglasses to see what was happening here. James wanted the brethren to see the harm they were doing in James 2:1-4, "My brethren, do not hold the faith of our Lord Jesus Christ, the Lord of glory, with partiality. For if there should come into your assembly a man with gold rings, in fine apparel, and there should also come in a poor man in filthy clothes, and you pay attention to the one wearing the fine clothes and say to him, "You sit here in a good place," and say to the poor men, You stand there or sit here at my footstool," have you not shown partiality among yourselves, and become judges with evil thoughts?" Is this not a stumbling block for others when they see the favoritism? I try very diligently to treat everyone in the same way, with respect and love. I wrote the following poem when I was examining my own heart.

The Beauty Within

Mirror, Mirror tell me true
How does my image look to you?
Can you see deep into my heart
Or can you only see just a part?
Do others see me as you do, only my face
Or do they see beauty beyond my surface?
I pray that the glow of my face
Will shine and show God's grace.
Deep within my heart I want to give love,
And be an example of God who is above.
Friends and loved ones are there to help me,
But only Christ can help me be all that I can be.
Whether it be a smile or a tear,
A note of compassion or a note of cheer,
When I can help another with charity,
Then the mirror will reflect
The beauty of Christ in me with clarity.
Barbara J. Barnes

Man looks on the outside, but God looks within. We read in 1 Samuel 16:7, "But the Lord said to Samuel, "Do not look at his appearance or at his physical stature, because I have refused him. For the Lord does not see as man sees; for man looks at the outward appearance, but the Lord looks at the heart." Others should see us as God sees us, a heart that is filled like unto Christ. No matter where we are or who we are with, people should always see our light shining for God. Others should be able to depend on us standing on the word of God. If people see us teaching one thing and practicing something else, it would be almost impossible for us to have a good influence on them. Again, Jesus said in the sermon on the mountain in Matthew 5:16 "Let your light so shine before men, that they may see your good works and glorify your Father in heaven."

Worksheet for Chapter 6

1. List some things that show there is a God.
2. We did not witness Christ, but we believe. Why do we believe?
3. How do we see our place in God's plan?
4. How do others see our faith? Or do others see our faith?
5. What should God see when He looks in our heart?
6. Is there something that hinders us from seeing our faith clearly?
7. How do we allow others to hinder us from being more faithful?
8. List some things that would help us become more faithful.

Always let the light of your love shine from a humble and forgiving heart.

"But as it is written: Eye has not seen, nor ear heard, nor have entered into the heart of man the things which God has prepared for those who love Him." 1 Corinthians 2:9

Chapter 7

The little lady searched for a second and then with a smile withdrew pen and paper.

Do you take the time to write down your favorite verses? Most all of us have certain scripture that hold special meaning in our heart. I know when I think of the hope in Christ I read Lamentations 3:22-24; "Through the Lord's mercies we are not consumed, because His compassions fail not, they are new every morning. Great is Your faithfulness, the Lord is my portion, says my soul, therefore I hope in Him!" Paul writes in Romans 15:4; "For whatever things were written before were written for our learning, that we through the patience and comfort of the Scriptures might have hope." Hebrews chapter eleven is often referred to as the hall of fame for the faithful. I get comfort from God's word in Hebrews 11:6; "But without faith it is impossible to please Him, for he who comes to

God must believe that He is, and that He is a rewarder of those who diligently seek Him."

When thinking of love, I remember John 3:16; "For God so loved the world that He gave His only begotten Son, that whoever believes in Him should not perish but have everlasting life." Then there is the verse we all know in 1 Corinthians 13:13; "And now abide in faith, hope, love, these three; but the greatest of these is love." **Love is what moves us to act on our faith with hope of heaven**. We need to share God's love with others and give them the opportunity to know Him and His great love. Sharing the life we live as Paul writes in 2 Corinthians 3:2, "You are our epistle written in our hearts, known and read by all men."

We are so blessed today because we have the written Word of God. Most of us have several copies of the Bible in our homes. We have a mission from God to reach all those who do not have this blessing. We read in Matthew 28:19-20; "Go therefore and make disciples of all the nations, baptizing them in the name of the Father and of the Son and of the Holy Spirit, teaching them to observe all things that I have commanded you; and lo, I am with you always even to the end of the age. Amen." I have been blessed in my life with five missionary trips and have had the privilege of teaching many young and older women the Word of God.

God can use us wherever we live or go. Women have many roles in life and sometimes the greatest way God can use us is with our families. God has given us instructions through Paul's inspired writings in 2 Timothy 3:16-17; "All Scripture is given by inspiration of God, and is profitable for doctrine, for reproof, for correction, for instruction in righteousness, that the man of God may be complete, thoroughly equipped, for every good work." Profitable for doctrine and reproof tells what is right and what is not right. Correction tells us one must get it right and the instruction of righteousness is how to stay right. **God's word provides all we need to live a life according to His will and to His glory**

Genesis 18:19, "For I have known him in order that he may command his children and his household after him, that they keep the way of the Lord, to do righteousness and justice, that the Lord may bring to Abraham what He has spoken to him," When I was young, we had memory verses and I can still recite most of them. However, in my golden years, it doesn't seem to be as easy. Therefore, I write or type the verses and post them where I can see them to refresh my mind of their meaning. I pray that the words of my mouth will be acceptable to our Father. I think of David as he wrote in Psalm 19:14, "Let the words of my mouth and the meditation of my heart be acceptable in Your sight, O

Lord, my strength and my Redeemer." This applies also for the words that I write for myself and others.

Pen and paper is always good to have nearby for jotting down those who need a special prayer, a card, or a phone call. Paul writes in Galatians 6:10; "Therefore, as we have opportunity, let us do good to all, especially to those who are of the household of faith." Taking time to write a card or make a call to someone could make a bad day turn into a good day. I love making cards for all occasions and sending to all those that come into my life. Once you are on my list, you are there to stay. This may not be your talent, but there are many inexpensive cards on the market and a phone call is very inexpensive. Let people know you are praying for them. Having someone say that my family is on their prayer list is so encouraging to me. When having trouble saying a prayer, write it down. This is a good way to go back and see that God has answered your request and then say a thank you prayer.

We sing a song that comes to mind, "Count your many blessings." It is amazing to see just how blessed we are when we write them down. Paul writes in Ephesians 1:3; "Blessed be the God and Father of our Lord Jesus Christ, who has blessed us with every spiritual blessing in the heavenly places in Christ." Thinking on all the blessings we have keeps us from dwelling on things we might not have or need. Write down ways that you can share with others the things you have been blessed with. Write down what it means for you to live for Christ. Let others know how you are blessed in Christ. Sharing your blessings may help others to become more aware of just how blessed they are.

Take notes in your Bible class. It stays with you longer and you can have the scripture to look up that was discussed. Study before class and make notes or questions that you would like to ask in class. Paul tells us to study in 2 Timothy 2:15; "Be diligent to present yourself approved to God, a worker who does not need to be ashamed, rightly dividing the word of truth." We are all at different levels of our spiritual life in Christ. Write down the things you feel you need to work on for a stronger faith.

Keeping a journal is very helpful. There are some I have finished and some I have not. Sometimes I only write a half a page, but I do try to write on a daily basis. When we write in our journal, we write from the heart and about the things that are most important to us. Seeing our words on paper sometimes will shed a new light on our thoughts. This will sometimes provoke us to study deeper in God's Word. We want to be true to the Word, whether we speak it or write it. "For as he thinks in his heart, so is he…" Proverbs 23:7. I love to sing the song, "Tell Me the Story of Jesus, write on my heart every word." Think about writing your thoughts in a song, or a poem, or write a book. When writing about God's love and grace your faith will be increased. I have received notes of encouragement from others that help me when I have down days. The preacher has something similar and he calls it his "make my day" box. We all need one.

Most everyone I know makes cue cards when making a speech or teaching a Bible class. Post it notes are great for a quick look to keep focused. This helps us to stay true to what we are trying to convey to our audience. When having a Bible study, reference cards are good, but make sure you have your Bible close so the person you are studying with can see what you are saying is true to the Word. It is good to have the person you are studying with look up the scripture; this helps them become more familiar with the Bible. Having them write the scripture will enable them to remember more than just reading it.

Teaching or leading a Bible study will increase your knowledge, this reminds me of the scripture in 2 Peter 1:5-8; "But also for this very reason giving all diligence, add to your faith virtue, to virtue knowledge, to knowledge self-control, to self-control perseverance, to perseverance godliness, to godliness brotherly kindness, and to brotherly kindness love, for if these things are yours and abound, you will be neither barren nor unfruitful in the knowledge of our Lord Jesus Christ."

There are many ways and means to communicate the gospel with others. We want to use whatever means we have to reach those we love and are praying for their salvation. This chapter is one way for those who have a difficult time talking with others. Preparation is the key in whatever way you choose to communicate. Writing down your thoughts and scripture lets you go over your notes and make changes. Talking with others does not give you a chance sometimes to explain in detail or depth what you are really trying to say. Of course, if talking is your best way, then maybe you could recite your notes and scripture in front of the mirror or with someone you feel comfortable with before talking with the person you are trying to win over for Christ. It is written in Matthew chapter four that every time Jesus was tempted, His answer was always the same "It is written." God wants us to know His word and be prepared at all times, to sow the seed to fight Satan.

Worksheet for Chapter 7

1. Write one verse on a card to memorize and recite at next lesson.
2. Why is it important to pray for family and others?
3. Send cards of encouragement especially to shut-ins and to our military.
4. What do you consider a blessing?
5. This Sunday take paper and pen to make notes of the message.
6. Write something in your journal or on paper for each day this week.
7. How does God work in our life?

Pray for the understanding of God's word. Pray for God to lead you in the best way to reach out to others; whether it is by talking with them or by writing to them. God has told us that He will fully equip us for every good work. We can trust in His word. We are commanded to seek the lost and to share the gospel. God's Word will convict the heart and He will add them to His church.

Philippians 4:19, "And my God shall supply all your need according to His riches in glory by Christ Jesus."

Chapter 8

The little lady slowly and very carefully withdrew a small frayed crocheted cross from her pocketbook with tears in her eyes. This was made and given to her from her mother many years ago.

What do you think of when you see a cross? It reminds me of the price that was paid for the remission of my sins. It reminds me of the grace, the love, and the forgiveness of God. Also it reminds me of the hope of eternal life for those of us who are obedient to His Word. We read in Romans 5:8, "But God demonstrates His own love toward us, in that while we were still sinners Christ died for us." I remember many years ago I wore a small cross around my neck that someone had given me. One of my uncles saw it and started questioning me. I quickly told him that the cross was for everyone who believed in God and wanted to live a Christian life. There is only one thing that should come to our mind when we see the cross, that is Christ and the sacrifice He made for the sins of all who are obedient to God's Word. Christ's death and resurrection reconciled man under God's grace and gives us a hope for an eternal home in heaven with Him. Do you think it was easy for God to allow His beloved Son to be nailed on the cross for our sins? Yet, as His children, when we ask with godly sorrow, He loves and forgives us. "In this is love, not that we loved God, but that He loved us, and sent His Son to be the propitiation for our sins."1 John 4:10.

To truly forgive is very hard under some circumstances. The greater the hurt the harder it is to forgive, especially a member of your family or a close friend. I think the hardest to forgive is a hurt against our children caused by another family member. I experienced this in my family and it took years to finally forgive the person who caused the hurt. I allowed the anger and bitterness to take away my joy and I was not in the right relationship with God. We find in Hebrews 12:15 these words, "Looking carefully lest anyone fall short of the grace of God; lest any root of bitterness springing up cause trouble, and by this many become defiled."

The cross reminds me that Christ died so I could have the forgiveness of the Father, but He also gave this commandment in Matthew 6:14-15, "For if you forgive men their trespasses, your heavenly Father will also forgive you, but if you do not forgive men their trespasses, neither will your Father forgive your trespasses." When I think of how much I want my Father to forgive me, then I know I must be forgiving of others, no matter how difficult. Unforgiveness holds us hostage. Poison doesn't just hurt those it is poured on, but it hurts the vessel it is stored in. This year for the first time in twelve years I sent a birthday card to the family member who had hurt my child. It freed me and brought great joy and peace in my heart with thankfulness to my Father who loves me enough to forgive me. I was especially glad that God granted time for me to see and pray with him before his death.

God wants my heart to be right and it is for my salvation that I forgive others. The only person that can make things right for me is me with God's help and not the person who caused the hurt. Holding onto the hurt does nothing against the one who hurt you. Pray that God will help you and those who cause you hurt.

Facing someone that you want to forgive or ask forgiveness of is very humbling. There are many ways to ask for forgiveness or to give forgiveness if you have difficulty in facing the person. The important thing is to do it. We are never more like God than when we love the unlovable.

Paul writes in 2 Corinthians 5:18-19, "Now all things are of God, who has reconciled us to Himself through Jesus Christ, and has given us the ministry of reconciliation, that is, that God was in Christ reconciling the world to Himself, not imputing their trespasses to them, and has committed to us the word of reconciliation." It can be in a letter or a note written from the heart with love. Solomon wrote it like this in Proverbs 25:11, "A word fitly spoken is like apples of gold in settings of silver." Solomon also wrote in Proverbs 18:19, "A brother offended is harder to win than a strong city, and contentions are like the bars of a castle." Pray to God for the right words and right attitude**. God is love and everything we do must be done with love.** "Love is the greatest thing that God can give us; for He Himself is love; and it is the greatest thing we can give to God." (Jeremy Taylor) What a blessing we receive from our Father when we make things right. Do not allow your anger or pride to jeopardize your salvation. Pray and ask others to pray also. We need to let others know when we need help. Question yourself as to whether it is pride or lack of love that prevents you from giving or asking for forgiveness.

In 1 Corinthians 13:5 it tells us that love does not seek its own. Holding onto grudges, anger, and bitterness will weaken our love and open our hearts for evil to enter.

Willard Tate's, *Habits of a Loving Heart,* shared a story which illustrates how a loving heart can truly forgive. The story begins with a young woman who, while in college, in the bright years of her life, was abducted by a man, raped, and murdered. Her killer was apprehended, convicted, and sentenced to prison. The girl's parents, rather than hating the man, started reaching out to him with letters offering love and forgiveness, attempting to teach him the truth of Christ's way. After trying for some time, they were finally granted an interview with him in prison, and they went to see him face to face. According to the book, the mother said that when they saw the man who had killed their daughter, they hugged him and cried and told him they had forgiven him. Paul writes in 2 Corinthians 5:17, "Therefore, if anyone is in Christ, he is a new creation; old things have passed away; behold, all things have become new." As amazing as that is, there's more to the story. Later, after the killer had committed his life to Christ, the girl's mother started traveling across the country, speaking about the joy and power of forgiveness, telling their story. How do you suppose her audiences responded? Were they overwhelmed with the faith and love of those parents? Did they rejoice over the salvation of a sin-darkened soul? No, when the audiences heard about those parents' attitude toward the man who had killed their daughter, they actually grew hostile toward the woman! What does that say about their hearts? How could they possibly forgive the man who had done such horrible things to their daughter? It was inexcusable, the people said—beyond comprehension. Rather than forgiving him, the parents should have pushed for the full punishment of the law. What do you think about this story? We are so quick to judge what others should or should not do that we rarely see our lack of doing the right thing. I know without a doubt I want the mercy and grace of God and not what I deserve. "In Him we have redemption through His blood, the forgiveness of sins, according to the riches of His grace." Ephesians 1:7. How can we show the love of God to others if we do not have it in our own heart? How can we lead others to Christ when they see the anger or bitterness in our lives?

Reading about King David's sorrow when he did wrong gives me comfort because God loved him, forgave him, and used him according to His purpose. One of my favorite prayers of David's is found in Psalm 51:10-13, "Create in me a clean heart, O God, and renew a steadfast spirit within me. Do not cast me away from Your presence and do not take Your Holy Spirit from me. Restore to me the joy of Your salvation, and uphold me with Your generous Spirit. Then I will teach transgressors Your ways, and sinners shall be converted to You." David realized that he had to be right with God before he could help others turn from their sins.

Others cannot always see our unforgiving heart, but if they are around us long enough it will become evident. When I think of the sin I try to hide I think of a tiny splinter in the tip of my finger that cannot be seen by the naked eye. Left unattended the splinter will become infected and swell and then it begins to hurt and get my attention. I can try to soothe it but if I still do not take the proper treatment, then it can develop blood poison and if continued not to be taken care of, it can lead to death. We read in 1 Corinthians 5:6, "Your glorying is not good. Do you not know that a little leaven leavens the whole lump?" That little tiny splinter can cause my whole body to die if not taken care of. Think about something that wasn't very important to you, but perhaps it was important to the other person. Whether we did the wrong or we received the wrong God tell us this in 1 Peter 3:17, "For it is better, if it is the will of God, to suffer for doing good than for doing evil." **May God help us to have the love it takes to make it right no matter who is in the wrong?** Paul writes in Romans 12:18, "If it is possible, as much as depends on you live peaceably with all men."

What is on the inside will always manifest itself where it can be seen by others. A man said when you squeeze the tube of toothpaste; toothpaste always comes out, not shaving cream, not face cream, but toothpaste. It always comes out toothpaste because that is what is on the inside. When we go through difficult times, pressure and/or a squeeze will cause whatever is inside to come out. Let's have love on the inside so that no matter what comes our way, love will always come out.

Worksheet for Chapter 8

1. What does the cross mean to you?
2. How do we handle a wrong?
3. Read and discuss Matthew 6:14-15.
4. List ways that will help us when we forgive others.
5. How can we help someone struggling with forgiveness?
6. Make a list of scriptures on forgiveness.

The cross could be an open door to start a conversation with someone. They could see your cross and say, 'oh, you must be a Christian' and then you could share your faith.

"If we say that we have no sin, we deceive ourselves, and the truth is not in us. If we confess our sins, He is faithful and just to forgive us our sins and to cleanse us from all unrighteousness."1 John 1:8-9

Chapter 9

She reached into a side pocket and withdrew a bookmark with the model prayer that Jesus gave us in Matthew 6:9-13.

"In this manner, therefore, pray; Our Father in heaven, Hallowed be Your name. Your kingdom come, Your will be done on earth as it is in heaven. Give us this day our daily bread. And forgive us our debts, as we forgive our debtors. And do not lead us into temptation, but deliver us from the evil one. For Yours is the kingdom and the power and the glory forever. Amen." Jesus was giving us the things we were to pray about when we pray, but not as some were praying as written in Matthew 6:7, "And when you pray, do not use vain repetitions as the heathen do. For they think that they will be heard for their many words." Trust God with honesty in your prayer. He knows your heart, He understands our hurts. If you are frustrated, tell God. Be sincere. Prayer is not an act for God because He knows our every thought. **Say the things that are truly on your heart.**

God tells us to pray without ceasing in 1 Thessalonians 5:17. Our life and attitude should always reflect our dependency upon God through our prayers. What a privilege God has given us through prayer. We can approach His throne through Christ and let our request be made known and know that He hears us. Paul wrote in Philippians 4:6, "Be anxious for nothing, but in everything by prayer and supplication, with thanksgiving, let your requests be made known to God."

We all need to set aside a quiet time for personal prayer with God. Jesus tells us how in Matthew 6:6, "But you, when you pray, go into your room, and when you have shut your door, pray to your Father who is in the secret place, and your Father who sees in secret will reward you openly." We must have a humble heart when we come before God. There are things on our heart that we only want God to know and hear. We pray for our inner weakness and struggles and for our will to be in accordance with God's will. We pray for God's forgiveness and to have the right relationship with Him. Pray for the strength to forgive those who hurt us. We are to be grateful for God sending Jesus, our Savior and Redeemer. Read Psalms and see how David poured out his heart to God in all the phases of his life and after being forgiven, he tried to never repeat that sin again. David had a repentant heart and he gave all the glory and praise to God. As I stated in a previous chapter one of my favorites is Psalm 51:10-12, "Create in me a clean heart, O God, and renew a steadfast spirit within me. Do not cast me away from Your presence, and do not take Your Holy Spirit from me."

If you are struggling with your prayer life, maybe you need to see what is hindering you, as Paul writes in 2 Corinthians 2:11, "lest Satan should take advantage of us; for we are not ignorant of his devices." There are many ways in which the evil one tries to hinder us and we need to be on our guard.

Most important of all, schedule your priorities so God is always first as, found in Matthew 6:33, "But seek first the kingdom of God and His righteousness, and all these things shall be added to you." We need to prepare, remove sin in our life, have faith, and not doubt. We must believe, must trust, and must forgive others to be right with God. Keep our daily schedule within reason. Jesus tells us in Luke 18:1, "Then He spoke a parable to them, that men always ought to pray and not lose heart." We do not lose heart when we are in constant communion with God.

Our spiritual health is much like our physical health. When we are sick we go to the doctor and have a checkup and maybe some tests. The doctor tells us our problem and gives us a prescription and instructions on getting better. If we choose not to follow the doctor's advice or take the medicine, then chances are we are not going to get better. Our spiritual illness or weaknesses is similar when we don't keep in prayer and go to the scriptures for renewed strength. Paul wrote in 2 Corinthians 4:16, "Therefore we do not lose heart. Even though our outward man is perishing, yet the inward man is being renewed day by day." David wrote in Psalm 46:1, "God is our refuge and strength, a very present help in trouble." **We need nourishment every day from God's Word.**

We start our little ones with simple prayers that they can memorize and say over and over until they become old enough to form their own words of praise for the Lord. These prayers usually occur when we eat and at bedtime. How sweet and innocent are their prayers and how they display their trust that God will hear and answer. Sometimes we forget to have that trust when we pray. Jesus said in Matthew 18:2-5, "Then Jesus called a little child to Him, set him in the midst of them, and said, 'Assuredly, I say to you, unless you are converted and become as little children, you will by no means enter the kingdom of heaven. Therefore whoever humbles himself as this little child is the greatest in the kingdom of heaven, whoever receives one little child like this in My name receives Me." In verse ten of the same chapter, Jesus says these words, "Take heed that you do not despise one of these little ones, for I say to you that in heaven their angels always see the face of My Father who is in heaven."

When children start using their own words, they may ask God to help their pets and other things on their mind, never discourage them, they will learn more as they grow and hear our prayers. My grandson told his teacher one Sunday morning that his Nana prayed all the time about everything. It made me happy to hear that. Teaching them to pray is so important, but also teaching them how to pray is important. **We must always show respect and reverence to God when we pray**.

There are many occasions when women of the church pray in public. It might be at a Ladies Day, ladies meeting, ladies tea, ladies class, or when you teach the younger children. We have wedding showers, baby showers, and ladies cookie exchange. I try to always have a prayer with ladies when visiting in the hospital, rehab, or nursing homes. Maybe you would like to do this with short prayers until you are more comfortable with a group. Try to clear your mind of those around you and talk to God, we are in His presence.

Jesus tells us in Matthew 18:20, "For where two or three are gathered together in My name, I am in the midst of them." Always pray before any occasion for God's strength. Start out with just a short prayer and build up your confidence. In my early years of school I would take a zero in my class before I would stand before my peers. I eventually took a speech class which helped me talk before an audience. Later with practice I became more confident praying before other ladies. I still like to know ahead if I am to pray.

I keep a prayer journal and write the names of those I am praying about to God. Having a journal helps keep me focused on the needs of others. Maybe this would help you. I heard one lady suggest that we pray aloud in our private prayer so that we are better able to pray in public.

We know we cannot be praying all the time as written in 1 Thessalonians 5:17, "pray without ceasing." Just like when we walk in the light as John writes in 1 John 1:7, "But if we walk in the light as He is in the light, we have fellowship with one another, and the blood of Jesus Christ His Son cleanses us from all sin." This is the way we live or practice our life. Prayer is the same way; **we need to live a prayerful life.**

"…The effective prayer of a righteous man can accomplish much." James 5:16b. How you pray is very important, you must pray believing. We must pray with humility. Our country is experiencing troubled times now and we see this verse passed around as to how we need to pray in 2 Chronicles 7:14, "If My people who are called by My name will humble themselves, and pray and seek My face, and turn from their wicked ways, then I will hear from heaven, and will forgive their sin and heal their land." We can believe this because Jesus said in Mark 10:27, "But Jesus looked at them and said, "With men it is impossible, but not with God; for with God all things are possible."

There are many scriptures on the postures of prayer. Moses wrote of lying prostrate in Deuteronomy 9:18; Elijah was sitting when he prayed in I Kings19:4, and David tells of bowing and kneeling in Psalm 95:6, "Oh come, let us worship and bow down; let us kneel before the Lord our Maker." Jesus gave instructions on whenever we stand to pray in Mark 11:25. Paul writes of kneeling before the Father in Ephesians 3:14 and Paul wrote in 1Timothy 2:8 of lifting holy hands. Your heart must be right no matter the posture.

Put thought into your prayer for whom and for why you are praying. Matthew writes in Matthew 26:41, "Watch and pray, lest you enter into temptation. The spirit indeed is willing, but the flesh is weak." Make sure to ask according to God's instructions as James tells us in James 1:5, "If any of you lacks wisdom, let him ask of God, who gives to all liberally and without reproach, and it will be given to him."

We must be in a right relationship with God, seeking repentance and a clear conscience. Peter writes in 1 Peter 3:12, "For the eyes of the Lord are on the righteous, and His ears are open to their prayers; but the face of the Lord is against those who do evil."

It is important that we pray for the will of God to be done. Jesus prayed for God's will in Luke 22:42, "saying, "Father, if it is Your will, take this cup from Me; nevertheless not My will, but Yours be done." These instructions are also given in Jesus' model prayer in Matthew 6:10, "Your kingdom come, Your will be done." God requires we must surrender all our heart, body, soul, and mind to His will.

We are to have faith as James writes in James 1:6, "But let him ask in faith, with no doubting, for he who doubts is like a wave of the sea driven and tossed by the wind." Jesus tells us a parable on not giving up in Luke 18:1-8. The widow went before the judge so many times with her petition that the judge finally granted her request

I pray every morning for the salvation of my children, even knowing that the choice is theirs to make. It is on my heart everyday so that I can be a better example before them as to how God blesses my life in Christ.

Read this phrase and thought it would fit into my lesson on prayer.

Happy moments, praise God
Difficult moments, seek God
Quiet moments, worship God
Painful moments, trust God
Every moment, thank God

Worksheet for Chapter 9

1. Do we have a sweet aroma in our prayers to God?
2. How do we humble ourselves before God?
3. How can we remove doubt from our prayer?
4. How can others affect our prayers?
5. How can we limit God's answer to our prayers?
6. Why is forgiveness for others important to our prayer life?
7. How do we show our thankfulness to God for His blessings?

"ASAP"

Always Say A Prayer

"In everything give thanks; for this is the will of God in Christ Jesus for you.
1 Thessalonians 5:18

Chapter 10

Next the little lady took out her medication prescription.

This chapter is about having a healthy spiritual relationship with God. Paul writes in 1 Corinthians 3:16, "Do you not know that you are the temple of God and that the Spirit of God dwells in you?" Mark wrote in Mark 7:20-23, "And He said, What comes out of a man, that defiles a man. For from within, out of the heart of men, proceed evil thoughts, adulteries, fornications, murders, thefts, covetousness, wickedness, deceit, lewdness, an evil eye, blasphemy, pride, foolishness. All these evil things come from within and defile a man." We can accomplish a fit physical body when we set our mind to the task. It is the same when getting spiritually fit in our heart and mind for the Lord. God's Word gives us not only a healthier physical way of life, but He gives us the way for a healthy spiritual life. Christ has paid the price for our prescription for a healthier and righteous relationship with God.

God has given us the formula for a healthy spiritual life in Galatians 5:22-23; "But the fruit of the Spirit is love, joy, peace, longsuffering, kindness, goodness, faithfulness, gentleness, self-control. Against such there is no law." Jesus says in Matthew 7:20; "Therefore by their fruits you will know them." Do you pray for at least one of these attributes to be improved in your life each day? Are you ready to accept what God sends you in order for your prayer to be answered? The following demonstration of this was sent in an e-mail. There came a great flood and the people were climbing upon their roofs for safety. This man prayed for God's help. A boat came by and the man was asked if he wanted a ride, but he said that he was waiting for God. Then another boat came by and the man refused a ride again. Then a helicopter flew over and yelled down to the man and he again said that he was waiting for God. The water continued to rise and the man eventually drowned. When the man saw God, he asks why God did not save him and God answered him, I sent you help three times and you refused each one. We have to realize that God does not work the same way as our thinking. Isaiah writes in Isaiah 55:8-9, "For My thoughts are not your thoughts, nor are your ways My ways," says the Lord. "For as the heavens are higher than the earth, so are My ways higher than your ways and My thoughts than your thoughts."

We often fail to see God's plan when we pray for God to give us the answer that we think would work best for us. **When we become a child of God, we make a commitment to surrender our will to God's will.** We are asked to make sacrifices and when we do, then all the "I want" must die and be replaced with "what God wants". To be spiritually healthy we must give up self. Paul wrote in Galatians 2:20, "I have been crucified with Christ; it is no longer I who live, but Christ lives in me, and the life which I now live in the flesh I live by faith in the Son of God, who loved me and gave Himself for me." Eating the wrong foods can cause our bodies to become unhealthy and develop all kinds of harmful diseases that could lead to death, just as sin can separate us from God and cause our spiritual death.

A spiritual death will bring these words that Jesus said in Matthew 7:23, "And then I will declare to them, I never knew you; depart from Me, you who practice lawlessness!" The answer to keeping a healthy and righteous relationship with God will be the words found in Revelation 2:10b, "Be faithful until death, and I will give you the crown of life." The word "until" in this verse means to have faith until death. The Christians were being tortured for their faith by

Romans and Jews. This verse was to give encouragement and assurance to the faithful.

Taking your medication when it is convenient for you will not properly heal you and may hinder the healing. Serving God when it is convenient for us will decay our spiritual life. Paul urges us in Romans 12:2, "And do not be conformed to this world, but be transformed by the renewing of your mind, that you may prove what is that good and acceptable and perfect will of God." We read in 2 Corinthians 4:16, "Therefore we do not lose heart, even though our outward man is perishing, yet the inward man is being renewed day by day." We need to remember that even though medicine helps us to feel better, it is only temporary and our body will decay. The renewing of the inner man comes from studying God's Word and serving Him which will give us eternal life.

We need to have a healthy relationship with God. When we are weary Paul writes in Galatians 6:9, "And let us not grow weary while doing good, for in due season we shall reap if we do not lose heart." When in need of comfort read 2 Corinthians 1:3-4, "Blessed be the God and Father of our Lord Jesus Christ, the Father of mercies and God of all comfort, who comforts us in all our tribulation, that we may be able to comfort those who are in any trouble, with the comfort with which we ourselves are comforted by God." Psalm 23 is another scripture when in need of comfort.

We must keep up the physical body to maintain our health; it is the same with our spiritual life flushing out the impurities of body and heart. If we have bitterness in our hearts it creates a dirty filter that every thought and emotion has to travel through. Read and apply Ephesians 4:31-32, "Let all bitterness, wrath, anger, clamor, and evil speaking be put away from you, with all malice, and be kind to one another, tender-hearted, forgiving one another, even as God in Christ forgave you." This will free your heart and restore your joy in Christ. When you need strength then read one of my favorites found in Philippians 4:13, "I can do all things through Christ who strengthens me." When we need help of any kind go to Psalm 121:1-2, "I will lift up my eyes to the hills, from whence comes my help? My help comes from the Lord, who made heaven and earth." Write down the verses that help you and keep them close or try to memorize so you can recite them when needed. Also, think about how Joseph forgave his brothers in Genesis 45:5, "But now, do not therefore be grieved nor angry with yourselves because you sold me here, for God sent me before you to preserve life." **We need to be a forgiving people.**

Just as there are so many ways in which our bodies can become unhealthy, there are so many ways we are tempted to sin in our spiritual life which separate us from God.

In Romans 8:35-39 through inspiration from God Paul writes, "Who shall separate us from the love of Christ? Shall tribulation, or distress or persecution, or famine, or nakedness, or peril, or sword? As it is written: "For Your sake we are killed all day long; we are accounted as sheep for the slaughter." Yet in all these things we are more than conquerors through Him who loved us. For I am persuaded that neither death nor life, nor angels nor principalities nor powers, nor things present nor things to come, nor height nor depth, nor any other created thing, shall be able to separate us from the love of God which is in Christ Jesus our Lord." It is we, ourselves, who allow the things of this world to separate us from the love of God.

We are given the formula or prescription by God to help in our spiritual health in His word. We find assurance of this in 2 Timothy 3:16-17, "All Scripture is given by inspiration of God, and is profitable for doctrine, for reproof, for correction, for instruction in righteousness, that the man of God may be complete, thoroughly equipped for every good work." If we fail to take the medication given by our doctor to make us well, we will continue to suffer and sometimes it could be fatal. The same is true with God's prescription for our spiritual life, if not obedient; we may not recover and lose our soul. God is the great physician of the soul.

I remember when I was young and my mother gave me cod liver oil, I thought I would forever be sick for it tasted so horrible, but my body needed it for strength. In our spiritual life we are going to have difficulties, trials, and tribulations at times seem hard to swallow or to understand. We need to place our faith in God's remedy. Romans 5:1-5, "Therefore, having been justified by faith, we have peace with God through our Lord Jesus Christ, through whom also we have access by faith into this grace in which we stand, and rejoice in hope of the glory of God. And not only that, but we also glory in tribulations, knowing that tribulation produces perseverance; and perseverance, character; and character, hope. Now hope does not disappoint, because the love of God has been poured out in our hearts by the Holy Spirit who was given to us." Hope is a great medication against sin. Sin will cause the destruction of our spiritual life. Live always with eternal hope in your heart

Others can help with our healing as James writes in James 5:14-16, "Is anyone among you sick? Let him call for the elders of the church, and let them pray over him anointing him with oil in the name of the Lord. And the prayer of faith will save the sick and the Lord will raise him up. And if he has committed sins, he will be forgiven. Confess your trespasses to one another, and pray for one another, that you may be healed. The effective, fervent prayer of a righteous man avails much." Physical medication will help the earthly body, but it cannot keep us physically alive forever. Only God's medication, His Word, can give us spiritual health and life eternally in heaven.

Worksheet for Chapter 10

1. How can we seek a healthier spiritual life?
2. Why should we search the scriptures for ourselves?
3. Name some of the benefits of reading scriptures daily.
4. Do we have friends that help us stay healthy in the Lord?
5. How can you help others with their spiritual health?
6. How healthy are we if we only ate as often as we read God's word?

Discussion:

What is the formula for keeping a
healthy relationship with God?

"I beseech you therefore, brethren, by the mercies of God that you present your bodies a living sacrifice holy acceptable to God, which is your reasonable service." Romans 12:1

Chapter 11

The little lady reached deep into her pocketbook and withdrew a hand full of coins.

"For God so loved the world that He gave His only begotten Son, that whoever believes in Him should not perish but have everlasting life." John 3:16. I really can't comprehend the great love that God has for us. Oh, to have some of the understanding of the Son who with complete obedience and willingness did the will of our Father and almighty God by coming to earth as a mortal and dying a cruel death on the cross for our sins, not His, but ours. There is nothing we can do to earn God's salvation; it is only because of His great love. Romans 5:8, "But God demonstrates His own love toward us, in that while we were still sinners, Christ died for us." David wrote in Psalm 49:8, "For the redemption of their souls is costly..." What God ask of us is so tiny compared to what was required of His Son. Jesus became the Son of man, the perfect sacrifice, and suffered a cruel death, the price required for our redemption. Paul wrote in 1 Corinthians 6:20, "For you were bought at a price, therefore glorify God in your body and in your spirit, which are God's."

Do we appreciate the help we receive from God and the cost that He has paid with the death of His Son for our redemption and hope of heaven? The Hebrews writer says this in Hebrews 2:9, "But we see Jesus, who was made a little lower than the angels, for the suffering of death crowned with glory and honor, that He, by the grace of God, might taste death for everyone." We only need to choose Him and He will supply all our needs as it is written in Matthew 6:33, "But seek first the kingdom of God and His righteousness, and all these things shall be added to you."

With the status of the economy these days, money is certainly on all our minds. The question of what is it going to cost enters into our thoughts every time we see something we would like to have. What can I do without so I can make this purchase? My daughter once witnessed a couple trying to decide which medicine they could afford although they needed all the prescriptions. Living on a fixed income has given me a new perspective to life in the financial scheme of things. I am not only blessed by God but He blesses me with a daughter who helps me out from time to time. I am so thankful for her. God has promised to give us what we need in Philippians 4:19, "And my God shall supply all your need according to His riches in glory by Christ Jesus." We are to remember that God provides our needs and not our greed.

Luke tells us in Luke chapter 14 that we must plan the cost of the building before we start the foundation if we are to be successful. It is the same in our spiritual life. Matthew 13:44, "Again, the kingdom of heaven is like treasure hidden in a field, which a man found and hid; and for joy over it he goes and sells all that he has and buys that field." Matthew 13:45-46, "Again, the kingdom of heaven is like a merchant seeking beautiful pearls, who, when he had found one pearl of great price, went and sold all that he had and bought it." These men thought the treasure was worth everything they had and they sacrificed all to obtain it. Do we sacrifice everything for the treasure of heaven? Do we do as little as possible and expect God to reward us with the greatest gift? God tells us in Matthew 6:21 and Luke 12:34, "For where your treasure is, there your heart will be also." As the man who found the treasure and was urgent in obtaining that treasure we need to do the same with God's word at all cost. The urgency is found in 2 Timothy 4:2-3a, "Preach the word! Be ready in season and out of season. Convince, rebuke, exhort, with all longsuffering and teaching. For the time will come when they will not endure sound doctrine."

Christ gives us this commandment in Matthew 28:19-20, "Go therefore and make disciples of all the nations, baptizing them in the name of the Father and the Son and the Holy Spirit, teaching them to observe all that I commanded you, and lo, I am with you always, even to the end of the age." We are commanded to share the Gospel with the entire world. There are many missionaries who go into countries where people have never heard the gospel. The missionaries go with the knowledge they could lose their life, which many have. They knew the cost and still went to give hope to those without hope. There are some who never have the opportunity to share the Word in other countries. We don't have to go around the world to teach the gospel to others. It is amazing so many in this country have never really learned about God's love and plan of salvation. We are still commanded to spread God's Word with everyone that comes into our lives. We can all teach the life of Christ and His ministry from the hope and blessings that are within our lives in Christ. Paul writes in Philippians 4:13, "I can do all things through Christ who strengthens me." We do not need a degree to teach the love that is in our heart for the Lord. The cost and greatness of

God's love has given us a value we could never obtain except through the obedience to His word. The obedience is our baptism into Christ's death, burial and resurrection for the forgiveness of our sins.

Do we sometimes feel like we are taken for granted by others? Really, can't anyone else do some of these things, why is it always me, like I have the time? Do I really sacrifice or do I just do it because I don't want to feel guilty about not doing it? Paul writes in Galatians 6:10, "Therefore, as we have opportunity; let us do good to all, especially to those who are of the household of faith." Do we see these times as opportunities that God is placing in our paths? It seems we have a much harder time saying yes to some of the things that inconvenience us, but have an easier time saying yes when it is at our convenience. Does saying yes only at our convenience constitute a sacrifice? We are to do good to everyone, but especially to our family in Christ. Jesus said in Matthew 5:16 "Let your light so shine before men that they may see your good works and glorify your Father in heaven." Good works done with love will take away any cost we might feel for sacrificing our time or money. Paul wrote in Romans 8:18, "For I consider that the sufferings of this present time are not worthy to be compared with the glory which shall be revealed in us."

We are to avoid the pleasures of the world which will lead to sin. This doesn't just happen, it is a process of daily denying our self. Paul wrote in 1 Corinthians 9:27, "But I discipline my body and bring it into subjection, lest, when I have preached to others, I myself should become disqualified." When we practice doing well, it becomes a way of life and we strive for the perfection of Christ. Jesus told the people and his disciples to take up His cross in Mark 8:34, "When He had called the people to Himself, with His disciples also, He said to them, whoever desires to come after Me, let him deny himself, and take up his cross and follow Me."

We who are in Christ are no longer our own. Paul wrote in I Corinthians 6:19-20, "Or do you not know that your body is the temple of the Holy Spirit who is in you, whom you have from God, and you are not your own? For you were bought at a price; therefore glorify God in your body and in your spirit, which are God's."

We are in a race and battle that has already been won by Christ and if we remain in Christ we win! God's Word tells us how to overcome the world in 1 John 5:4-5, "For whatever is born of God overcomes the world. And this is the victory that has overcome the world – our faith. Who is He who overcomes the world, but he who believes that

Jesus is the Son of God?" Our faith needs to be strong and sacrificial like the first believers as Paul wrote in Hebrews 11:36-38, "Still others had trial of mockings and scourgings, yes, and of chains and imprisonment. They were stoned, they were sawn in two, were tempted, were slain with the sword. They wandered about in sheepskins and goatskins, being destitute, afflicted, tormented – of whom the world was not worthy. They wandered in deserts and mountains, in dens and caves of the earth." Paul said of himself in Philippians 3:8, "Yet indeed I also count all things loss for the excellence of the knowledge of Christ Jesus my Lord, for whom I have suffered the loss of all things, and count them as rubbish, that I may gain Christ."

Jesus gave praise to the widow with the two mites, which are very small copper coins worth a fraction of a penny in Mark 12:42-44, "Then one poor widow came and threw in two mites, which make a quadrans. So He called His disciples to Himself and said to them, Assuredly, I say to you that this poor widow has put in more than all those who have given to the treasury; for they all put in out of their abundance, but she out of her poverty put in all that she had, her whole livelihood." When you really think about this widow who had no husband, family, income, Social Security, or "mailbox money" giving all that she had showed an example of true faith. **Her giving truly reflected her trust in God.**

When we suffer unto righteousness then it is well pleasing to God. All that we do needs to be to the glory of God. Nothing goes unnoticed by God or those around us, good or bad. Others are watching how we cope with the trials and temptations we face each day. Let's demonstrate to them our trust in God. Nothing we sacrifice compares to what Jesus sacrificed.

Worksheet for Chapter 11

1. What value do we place on the cost of our salvation?
2. How does our sacrifice compare to the sacrifice of Christ?
3. Do we purpose our income?
4. Does our giving reflect God first in our life?
5. Do we have the same trust the widow had in her giving?

Discussion

How do we spread the Word of God and to whom?

"For what profit is it to a man if he gains the whole world, and loses his own soul? Or what will a man give in exchange for his soul?

Matthew 16:26

Chapter 12

The little lady looked again into her purse and withdrew a small mirror. "Oh my, what must I look like", she exclaimed.

Looking into a mirror will show our physical image. It will tell us if our image is okay for the way we want to look for ourselves and others. We look for any imperfections or flaws in our physical appearance that would keep us from looking our best. We should have the same desire of the heart with our Christian appearance. We know that we are special women because we read in Genesis 1:26a, "Then God said," Let Us make man in Our image, according to Our likeness." How special does this make us feel, being made in the image of God?

Of course we know we do not look physically like God. God is Spirit as John wrote in John 4:24; "God is Spirit, and those who worship Him must worship in spirit and truth." He is not flesh as we are, but He gave us His spirit and a free will so that we would desire to worship Him, our Creator.

He has given us the ability to reason and to understand above all His other creations.

Paul begins his list in Galatians with love and all the things that make for a godly and transformed heart. The image and spirit we are to reflect as Christian women is found in Paul's writings in the book of Galatians 5:22-23; "But the fruit of the Spirit is love, joy, peace, longsuffering, kindness, goodness, faithfulness, gentleness, self-control. Against such there is no law." Love is so very important in our lives because we know that God is love as John wrote in 1 John 4:8, "He who does not love does not know God, for God is love." We know love is important from Paul's inspired words in 1 Corinthians 13:13; "And now abide faith, hope, love, these three; but the greatest of these is love." Our image should reflect the love of God in our hearts.

This is the fruit a Christian should bear:

1. Love; powerful attraction to another Webster
   - A. Agape (Greek): This is the love we are to have for God. Matthew 22:37-39; "Jesus said to him, "You shall love the Lord your God with all your heart, with all your soul, and with all your mind. This is the first and great commandment. And the

second is like it; "You shall love your neighbor as yourself."

1 John 4:19; "We love Him because He first loved us."

B. Phileo love is the love for one another, brotherly love.

C. Eros love is usually thought of as for husband and wife.

2. Joy; intense happiness within

   Romans 14:17, "For the kingdom of God is not eating and drinking, but righteousness and peace and joy in the Holy Spirit."

3. Peace; calm and contentment

   John 14:27, "Peace I leave with you, My peace I give to you; not as the world gives do I give to you. Let not your heart be troubled, neither let it be afraid."

   Philippians 4:7, "And the peace of God, which surpasses all understanding, will guard your hearts and minds through Christ Jesus."

4. Longsuffering; patient

    James 5:7-8a, "Therefore be patient, brethren until the coming of the Lord. See how the farmer waits for the precious fruit of the earth, waiting patiently for it until it receives the early and later rain. You also be patient."

    2 Peter 3:9, "The Lord is not slack concerning His promise, as some count slackness, but is longsuffering toward us, not willing that any should perish but that all should come to repentance."

5. Kindness; in a kind way – graciously – favorably

    Ephesians 2:7, "That in the ages to come He might show the exceeding riches of His grace in His kindness toward us in Christ Jesus."

    2 Peter 1:7, "to godliness brotherly kindness, and to brotherly kindness love."

This reminds me of what Mark Twain said; "Kindness is the language that deaf can hear and the blind can see."

6. Goodness; the state or quality of being good

   Psalm 23:6, "Surely goodness and mercy shall follow me all the days of my life; and I will dwell in the house of the Lord forever."

   Romans 2:4, "Or do you despise the riches of His goodness, forbearance, and longsuffering, not knowing that the goodness of God leads you to repentance?"

7. Faithfulness; belief – confidence – loyalty – religion

   Lamentations 3:22-24, "Through the Lord's mercies we are not consumed, because His compassions fail not, they are new every morning; Great is Your faithfulness. The Lord is my portion says my soul, therefore I hope in Him!"

This passage in Lamentations is one of my favorites.

8. Gentleness; meek – mild in manner or effect

   Ephesians 4:2, "with all lowliness and gentleness, with longsuffering bearing with one another in love."

   1 Peter 3:4, "but let it be the hidden person of the heart, with the incorruptible beauty of a gentle

and quiet spirit, which is very precious in the sight of God."

9. Self-Control; ability to refrain or restrain one's impulses, to hold back

   1 Peter 3:10, "For he who would love life and see good days, let him refrain his tongue from evil, and his lips from speaking deceit."

This is like the horse that allows a rider to have control over his movements, submitting his will to the riders. We are commanded to submit our will to the will of God completely.

We always talk about the five steps to become a Christian; hear, believe, repent, confess and be baptized for the remission of our sins. Do we talk enough about the eight steps that helps us to mature and stay faithful until death?

Peter writes about the attributes or image of these eight steps in which a Christian is to reflect in 2 Peter 1:5-7, "But also for this very reason, giving all diligence, add to your faith virtue, to virtue knowledge, to knowledge self-control, to self-control perseverance, to perseverance godliness, to godliness brotherly kindness, and to brotherly kindness love."

1. Faith – Belief – Trust

   1 Corinthians 16; 13-14, "Watch, stand fast in the faith, be brave, be strong. Let all that you do be done with love."

2. Virtue – Morality

   James 1:27, "Pure and undefiled religion before God and the Father is this; to visit orphans and widows in their trouble, and to keep oneself unspotted from the world."

3. Knowledge – State of Knowing

   Colossians 1:10, "that you may have a walk worthy of the Lord, fully pleasing Him, being fruitful in every good work and increasing in the knowledge of God."

4. Self-Control – To Refrain or Restrain one's Impulses

   1 Peter 3:10, "For he who would love life and see good days, let him refrain his tongue from evil, and his lips from speaking evil."

5. Perseverance – Persist in Spite of Obstacles

   Ephesians 6:18, "praying always with all prayer and supplication in the Spirit, being watchful to the end with all perseverance and supplication for all the saints."

6. Godliness – Devout

   1 Timothy 4:8, "For bodily exercise profits a little, but godliness is profitable for all things, having promise of the life that now is and of that which is to come."

7. Brotherly Kindness – Gracious to Others

   Romans 12:10, "Be kindly affectionate to one another with brotherly love, in honor giving preference to one another."

8. Love – Powerful Emotion for Another

   1 John 4:7, "Beloved, let us love one another, for love is of God; and everyone who loves is born of God and knows God."

Practicing these attributes will help to strengthen and keep Satan from entering into our lives. Our conduct should always reflect who we are and whose we are, the Lord's. Let us not be like the man in James 1:23-24, "For if anyone is a hearer of the word and not a doer, he is like a man observing his natural face in a mirror; for he observes himself, goes away and immediately forgets what kind of man he was."

Practicing these attributes will help us remain faithful. The image of God we reflect in our lives will help someone else see the need for Christ in their life.

We are made in the image of God let us not ever forget that.

Worksheet for Chapter 12

1. What do we see or think when we see our reflection in the mirror?
2. How are we special in God's sight?
3. Do we see God's image in us with confidence?
4. What fruit of the Spirit do you feel you need to improve the most?
5. What step(s) in 2 Peter 1:7 do you need to add to your Christian life?
6. Name some verses that help us keep our image reflecting God's image.

Discussion:

God created women with a special purpose. Does our image reflect God's love and purpose? How?

"In all things showing yourself to be a pattern of good works; in doctrine showing integrity, reverence, incorruptibility." Titus 2:7

Chapter 13

The little lady's pocket book was empty and so she started to put everything back remembering each item and how she had used them to God's glory.

She gently rubbed her hand worn Bible -
Teach God's inspired word.

The reward for teaching God's Word is we learn more than we teach. We are all at a different level in our spiritual life. It takes more time for some to reach their goals than others. Ask help from someone you are comfortable with to help you with a study if you need help. Pray always and read the Bible at every opportunity. Remember it is up to us to make sure we take time to read God's Word daily. Think of the times when waiting for something or someone and use that time to study, especially at the doctor's office. We should never become discouraged when we have not met our time frame, after all, our day can change and we may have to rearrange our priorities. Just never give up because God will never give up on us. Paul writes in Philippians 1:6, "Being confident of this very thing, that He who has begun a good work in you will complete it until the day of Jesus Christ." We need to make sure the lesson being taught will be on the level of the one we are teaching. Always pray for God's help and then thank Him when we have completed the Bible study.

Her keys reminded her of the keys to the Kingdom

Our keys are cut and made to fit a certain lock and only that key will open that lock. When we try to fit the scriptures like children work a puzzle, the edges become ragged and out of shape by trying to fit them where they do not belong. It is very important that we do not take scripture out of context because the lesson can be lost. We do not have to know all the scriptures of the Bible to study with someone as long as we teach the truth.

Remember that "no one cares how much you know until they know how much you care." We must be sincere and caring in our teaching. Many times we are told to use key words or thoughts to remember names or information. Getting in the habit of thinking how we are to respond to someone when we have the opportunity is well worth the effort. The joy it brings to others will give us inspiration to continue passing on the good news to all we meet. **God is always there for us**. "I can do all things through Christ who strengthens me." Philippians 4:13.

Looking at her family photos - Teaching
those we love the most:

First we must have the love of God in our hearts to teach those we love, His love. We press on to the goal of heaven as Paul writes in Philippians 3:14. It can be children teaching parents or parents teaching children. We read about Cornelius and how he and his entire household believed and were baptized into Christ after hearing the word preached by Peter in Acts chapter ten. Children are a great gift to parents and the greatest gift we parents can give our children is to be an example of God's love in which they can embrace Ephesians 6:4, "And you, fathers, do not provoke your children to wrath, but bring them up in the training and admonition of the Lord."

Photos of friends who had touched her life –
Sharing God's word:

We learn early in life the acronym "J O Y" which means, Jesus, Others and You. We make many friends and acquaintances in our lifetime and we need to use every opportunity to share the gospel with them. Some friends are closer than family as David wrote in Proverbs17:17a, "A friend loves at all times." Our friends in Christ are our most cherished friends. We find in Proverbs 18:24, "A man who has friends must himself be friendly, but there is a friend who sticks closer than a brother." Remember it is our mission to seek and teach the lost, God will do the saving.

Small pendant watch – Always take
time to share the Gospel:

Praying and thinking about doing good is good. Are we taking the time to follow through on it? Let us be more like the Christians in Berea as Luke writes in Acts 17:11, "… they received the word with all readiness, and searched the Scriptures daily to find out whether these things were so." They were diligent in their search taking the time to know if things taught were true to God's Word. We are not just to read but to ransack, turn it upside down, and inside out. Know exactly what God is saying to us. Read Matthew 12:3; 12:5; 19:4; and 22:31. These are scriptures that relate how powerful our time with God needs to be. **Don't let Satan rob us of the joy in our heart by neglecting our worship time with God, time with our family, time with friends, and time for our self.**

Her eye glasses – Seeing with the heart:

Can we see God? We cannot see the wind, but we know it is there because we see the results and action that it causes. When someone accepts Christ into their heart, we can see the change this brings into their life. Our life becomes Christ centered, not just a part, but of every aspect of our life. We are to have a humble and repentant heart to shine our light so others can see Christ in our lives and glorify the Father, Matthew 5:16.

Pen and paper – Studying the written word:

Do we have God's Word written in our heart? Inspired by God, Moses wrote in Deuteronomy 6:6-7, "And these words which I command you today shall be in your heart, you shall teach them diligently to your children, and shall talk of them when you sit in your house, when you walk by the way, when you lie down, and when you rise up." Peter wrote in 2 Peter 3:18, "But grow in the grace and knowledge of our Lord and Savior Jesus Christ. In Him be the glory both now and forever. Amen."

Crocheted bookmark cross - Christ's Sacrifice:

God offers His love and the way of salvation through His Son, Jesus the Christ, for all who are obedient to His Word. It is the blood of Jesus that now saves us from sin and the separation from God. Only in Christ can we have forgiveness from God. When we have godly sorrow and repent, God forgives us. We are to have a forgiving heart for those who trespass against us. In Matthew 18:21-22, Jesus told Peter that we are to forgive seventy times seven. **A forgiving heart with love does not keep a count of wrongs.** When God forgives, He blots out the sin.

Bookmark of Jesus model prayer - Our prayer life:

Prayer is our only communication with God. Christ gave many examples of His prayer life to God for us to follow. There are two important aspects to prayer. First is the sovereignty of God as we read in Isaiah 46:9 and the second aspect is our faith in prayer. There is a song we sing, What a Friend we have in Jesus, that reminds us of the importance of prayer in our life, Teach your children early the importance of a prayer life.

Medication - Keeping healthy Spiritual lives:

Our body is to be presented as a living sacrifice, holy and acceptable to God as Paul wrote in Romans 12:1. We are to keep our bodies as healthy as possible so we can do the will of God. We are to keep ourselves unspotted from the world, in the world, but not of the world. We are to put on the whole armor of God found in Ephesians 6:13-18. We are to find grace in time of need in Hebrews 4:16. We are to hope in Him in Lamentations 3:22-24; rejoice in Him in Romans 12:12, and anchor our soul in Him in Hebrews 6:19. Stay in the Word, not in the world.

Coins – Value of Our Redemption:

What is our worth? Most of the time people are asking about our finances as the world measures worth. Christian value is not determined by the world, our value comes from the ransom paid by Christ on the cross for our sins. Our riches and worth is beyond any measure the world can offer. The Son of God paid the price for our redemption and we are no longer slaves of sin, but have hope for heaven as Paul wrote in Galatians 4:7, "Therefore you are no longer a slave but a son, and if a son, then an heir of God through Christ." We are valuable in Christ and through His blood worthy to be a child of God.

Mirror - Reflecting the image of God:

There are many watching the way we live and the image we project. The influence or reflection we display can either encourage or discourage others. We need to build up and edify one another because each of us is created in the image of God. Paul wrote in 2 Corinthians 5:20, "Now then, we are ambassadors for Christ, as though God were pleading through us; we implore you on Christ's behalf, be reconciled to God." Our image should reflect the love of God in our hearts.

Empty pocket book – Remembrance:

Let us remember the characteristics of the new man in Christ as found in Colossians 3:12-17, "Therefore, as the elect of God, holy and beloved, put on tender mercies, kindness, humility of mind, meekness, longsuffering; bearing with one another, and forgiving one another, if anyone has a complaint against another; even as Christ forgave you, so you also must do. But above all these things put on love, which is the bond of perfection. And let the peace of God rule in your hearts, to which also you were called in one body; and be thankful. Let the word of God dwell in you richly in all wisdom, teaching and admonishing one another in psalms and hymns and spiritual songs, singing with grace in your hearts to the Lord. And whatever you do in word or deed, do all in the name of the Lord Jesus, giving thanks to God the Father through Him."

Paul by the inspired word of God wrote in 2 Timothy 4:7-8; "I have fought the good fight, I have finished the race. I have kept the faith. Finally, there is laid up for me the crown of righteousness, in which the Lord, the righteous Judge will give to me on that Day, and not to me only but also to all who have loved His appearing."

May we all run the race and be found faithful to receive the crown of righteousness.

Worksheet for Chapter 13

1. Discuss some ways we can teach God's Word to others.
2. How are we sharing God's Word with others?
3. Discuss how we encourage our family for Christ.
4. When do we schedule time for Bible study?
5. How can we keep our heart pure?
6. What kind of prayer life should we have?
7. List ways we can improve our spiritual life.

Discussion:

Discuss the ways we reflect the image of God to the unbelievers.

Discuss the ways we reflect the image of God to those who believe.

"But above all these things put on love, which is the bond of perfection." Colossians 3:14

Epilogue

My prayer is that each of you who read and study my book will glean something helpful within your own life. Maybe you will look at the things you carry in your pocketbook in a much different way. Christ spoke in parables to His followers so they could understand what He was teaching. We can read and see the spiritual meaning that each parable represented not only to them but also to us. God has given us many earthly talents that are helpful for us to reach others with His word. Our talents may not be the same and that is good because we will be reaching out to many different people as we share the plan of salvation giving God the glory.

God will supply us with everything we need to reach others. We need to be prepared to meet these opportunities and challenges when they come into our life. Are we so tied up in looking at our own selves that we fail to see the need of others? Sometimes we only get one chance. Are we living a life that reflects our love for God and Jesus? Many times I have failed, but one thing is for sure, God will never give up on me or you. We need to ask for His forgiveness and then 'shake it off' as the coaches tell the young athletes when they mess up. We only fail when we give up and not take it to the Lord. Singing the song, 'You Never Mention Him to Me', always brings tears to my eyes and my prayer is that from this point on in my life, no one can say that to me when this life ends. God be with you and may you be in Him.

Thank you for reading and or studying my book.

All the glory goes to God.

About the Author

Barbara lives in Florida. She is a member of the Pleasant Grove church of Christ in Inverness, Florida. Barbara has been on five missionary trips; she has traveled to Ghana, West Africa four times and hopes to return again. She helps with teaching grades three through fifth on Sunday mornings and Ladies Class on Wednesday night. She has been a speaker for Ladies Day and enjoys being a part of church activities. Barbara has been active in the Lads to Leaders/Leaderettes program. This is Barbara's first book but another one is in the works. Barbara is a veteran of the Air Force. She loves teaching and writing. Barbara is the mother of 2 children and lives close to her daughter Jennifer and grandchildren. You can contact her at barnesbj@yahoo.com.

Printed in the United States
By Bookmasters